PHARMACEUTICAL SUPPLY CHAIN ASSESSMENT FOR SRI LANKA

MARCH 2025

ASIAN DEVELOPMENT BANK

6 ADB Avenue, Mandaluyong City, 1550 Metro Manila, Philippines
Tel +63 2 8632 4444; Fax +63 2 8636 2444
www.adb.org

ISBN 978-92-9277-233-8 (print); 978-92-9277-234-5 (PDF); 978-92-9277-235-2 (ebook)
Publication Stock No. TCS250093-2
DOI: http://dx.doi.org/10.22617/TCS250093-2

Note:
In this publication, "$" refers to United States dollars and "SLR" refers to Sri Lanka rupees.

Cover design by Joe Mark Ganaban.

CONTENTS

TABLES, FIGURES, BOXES, AND CASE HIGHLIGHTS

TABLES

FIGURES

BOXES

CASE HIGHLIGHTS

ACKNOWLEDGMENTS

This report and assessments were prepared by an assessment team from the Asian Development Bank (ADB) under the guidance of the Ministry of Health (MOH) and the Ministry of Finance (MOF) of the Government of Sri Lanka. Much gratitude is due to several development partners including the World Health Organization (WHO), United Nations Children's Fund (UNICEF), and World Bank, which took part in and supported this assessment in various capacities. The High-Level Technical Working Group (TWG) comprised of experts from relevant government units, development partners, and representatives from industry and professional associations in Sri Lanka provided overall guidance and leadership to this assessment. The data collectors and members of the TWG are much appreciated for their wholehearted support. Valuable support and cooperation were likewise received from the key informants, focus group discussion participants, and health facilities that the assessment team visited.

The assessment team was led by Hasibul Haque, ADB senior pharmaceutical supply chain consultant, and co-led by Shalutha Athauda, pharmaceutical industry consultant, under the supervision of Dai- Ling Chen, health specialist. The ADB team members include Herathbanda Jayasundera, senior social development officer; Kumari Navaratne, senior public health consultant; and Nayana Fernando, public health consultant. Uhjin Kim, regional advisor—Essential Drugs and Medicines, WHO Regional Office for Southeast Asia; Sapumal Dhanapala, national professional officer—Emergency Risk Management, WHO Country Office for Sri Lanka; Innocent Dube, supply chain manager, UNICEF Supply Division; Wisdom Dube, supply chain systems strengthening consultant, UNICEF Supply Division; Mohan Wickramasinghe, supply and logistics officer, UNICEF Country Office for Sri Lanka; Kasun Rambukwella, registrar—Medical Administration, MOH; and Asita de Silva, ADB senior pharmacologist consultant provided comments and contributions as technical reviewers at various stages of the report.

All units including the National Medicines Regulatory Authority, Medical Supplies Division of MOH, State Pharmaceutical Corporation, and National Medicine Quality Assurance Laboratory extended their full support to the assessment. The support and guidance from the National Planning Department of MOF is greatly appreciated. The cooperation from the private sector including manufacturers, importers, and third party logistics providers contributed significantly. Finally, participants of the National Consultation Workshop including the Honorable Minister of Health, Secretary of Health, Director General of Health Services, Additional Secretaries of MOH—Procurement, Development, Medical Services, and Pharmaceuticals are gratefully acknowledged for their valuable time and contribution.

ABBREVIATIONS

ADB	Asian Development Bank
AMR	antimicrobial resistance
API	active pharmaceutical ingredient
ASEAN	Association of Southeast Asian Nations
CTD	common technical dossier
DGHS	Director General of Health Services
DMS	Department of Management Services
EML	Essential Medicine List
ERP	enterprise resource planning
FGD	focus group discussion
GS1	Global Standards 1
HRH	Human Resources for Health
HTA	Health Technology Assessment
ICH	International Council on Harmonization
KII	key informant interview
MEC	Medicine Evaluation Committee
MOH	Ministry of Health
MSD	Medical Supplies Division
NDTC	National Drug Therapeutic Committee
NMQAL	National Medicine Quality Assurance Laboratory
NMRA	National Medicines Regulatory Authority
NSCA	national supply chain assessment
PMCU	primary medical care unit
PSS	pharmaceutical system strengthening
QMS	Quality Management System
RMSD	Regional Medical Supplies Division
SLACPT	Sri Lanka Association of Clinical Pharmacology and Therapeutics
SLPMA	Sri Lanka Pharmaceutical Manufacturers Association
SLR	Sri Lankan rupee
SPC	State Pharmaceutical Corporation
SPMC	State Pharmaceutical Manufacturing Corporation
TOR	terms of reference
TWG	technical working group
UNICEF	United Nations Children's Fund
WHO	World Health Organization

WEIGHTS AND MEASURES

IU	international unit
mcg	microgram
mg	milligram
ml	milliliter

EXECUTIVE SUMMARY

Background. The pharmaceutical supply chain consists of all structures, people, resources, processes, and their interactions within the broader health system and market ecosystem. It seeks to ensure equitable and timely access to safe, effective, quality-assured pharmaceutical products and related services. An effective and efficient pharmaceutical supply chain promotes the appropriate and cost-effective use of pharmaceuticals to improve health outcomes. Sri Lanka's pharmaceutical supply chain consists of the Ministry of Health (MOH); National Medicines Regulatory Authority (NMRA) including the National Medicine Quality Assurance Laboratory (NMQAL), Medical Supplies Division (MSD), State Pharmaceutical Corporation (SPC), and State Pharmaceutical Manufacturing Corporation (SPMC); local importers; and manufacturers. They have helped to ensure that the pharmaceuticals provided served the country well in the past in achieving commendable health outcomes compared to other countries of the same economic level.

In the current structure, NMRA is responsible for regulation of pharmaceuticals to ensure the quality and safety of medicines and pharmaceutical products. Central procurement and supply of medicines, surgical items, consumables, diagnostics, and devices for all provincial and centrally managed health facilities fall under the purview of the central MOH with the MSD of MOH initiating and leading the process. The SPC serves as the procurement agent for the MSD. The forecasting, distribution, and monitoring of supplies are overseen by the MSD, in collaboration with 26 regional MSDs and based on an annual call for estimation of requirements from each hospital in the country.

Since 2019, a series of events including the easter bomb attack in 2019, the coronavirus disease (COVID-19) pandemic from 2020 to 2022, and the economic crisis from 2021 to 2023 have had major effects on MOH's pharmaceutical supply chain. This has led to associated stock-out issues and exposed some vulnerabilities and areas of improvement in the pharmaceutical supply chain system in Sri Lanka. These include issues in the areas of pharmaceutical supply chain governance, product registration system, forecasting, procurement process, storage and distribution, information system, rational use of medicines, staff shortage, and technical capacities.

Against this backdrop, the MOH and the Ministry of Finance, with support from the Asian Development Bank and other development partners, undertook an assessment from September 2023 to May 2024 aimed at fostering a comprehensive understanding of the Sri Lanka's pharmaceutical supply chain, identifying barriers, and analyzing improvement options.

Methodology. The mixed-methods approach employed for this assessment covered the areas of regulatory systems and quality assurance, appropriate use of medicines, medicines access, procurement and supply chain management, governance, human resources, information systems, and the market ecosystem. Data collection methods included desk reviews, assessment of facilities based on stratified random sampling across the whole country, patient satisfaction surveys, key informant interviews, focus group discussions, and a national consultation workshop. Data were analyzed qualitatively and quantitatively according to the conceptual areas.

Findings. Results show that thanks to the presence of a government health facility within a 5-kilometer reach by the population, as well as provisions for free medicines, Sri Lanka has attained high accessibility and affordability of medical products contributing to high patient satisfaction. Further, pharmaceuticals and supplies were fully funded by the Government of Sri Lanka, except during 2023 and 2024 when donor financing was requested to meet the funding shortfall to purchase pharmaceuticals. Sri Lanka's achievement of health indicators, commitment to free and equitable health care services, and resilience in recovering from the COVID-19 pandemic offer valuable lessons for countries with similar economic conditions.

As Sri Lanka recovers from the effects of the economic crisis, there are areas that can further improve the efficiency and effectiveness of the pharmaceutical supply chain. These include areas related to governance, procurement, rational use of medicines, logistics systems, fund flow, enhanced data analytics, quality assurance, capacity building and market shaping, which are detailed below.

(i) ***Governance.*** The MOH is responsible for overall governance of the pharmaceutical supply chain and its performance monitoring. Overall, the roles of procurement and logistics management are segregated between SPC and MSD respectively, but MSD directly manages procurement under the buyback agreements with SPMC and other local manufacturers. The roles of technical standards setting, policy making, and oversight are led by technical committees including NMRA but are not clearly segregated with a mechanism for ensuring accountability. This creates a vulnerability for the pharmaceutical supply chain that can be affected by possible external interference and corruption.

(ii) ***Procurement.*** The long lead time for forecasting, procurement, and supply is making it increasingly challenging to improve forecasting accuracy, align procurement with the annual budgetary cycle, and prepare realistic supply plans. Improving the process of forecasting, reducing the long procurement lead time by using appropriate procurement strategies, digitization, and supply planning would contribute to more efficient procurement, avoid shortage of supply, and help achieve lower prices for medicines.

(iii) ***Rational use of medicines.*** The National List of Essential Medicines (EML) of Sri Lanka that includes 383 medicines was firstly published in 2013-2014 and further revised in 2021. In 2023, a "priority list of medicines" of about 850 items were also adopted in parallel. However, compared to global and regional standards, both lists should be further reduced. The two lists should also be consolidated to avoid duplication and confusion. This requires changes in the institutional mechanisms to further rationalize product selection based on the principles of medicine optimization to achieve maximum therapeutic efficacy, minimum product variations, and optimum cost-effectiveness. Enhancing the rational use of medicines, optimizing product selection, aligning national treatment guidelines, and having an EML would reduce the need for procuring increased numbers of medicine variations, consolidate the demands in a relatively small medicines market, and achieve greater economies of scale.

(iv) ***Logistics system.*** The current storage and distribution network is not optimized for operational efficiency or for a predictable level of delivery service to the health facilities. Optimizing the storage and distribution network for direct delivery to health facilities and reducing the tiers in the supply chain would shorten delivery lead time, reduce the risk of quality loss, and minimize stock holding costs.

(v) ***Funds flow.*** During the economic crisis period, the pharmaceutical supply chain suffered from a lack of predictable funding and available foreign currency leading to a series of emergency decisions. Aligning procurement of pharmaceuticals to the annual allocation of the necessary funding and with assuring predictable release of funds are preconditions to stabilizing and improving the pharmaceutical supply chain in the postcrisis period.

(vi) ***Enhanced data analytics.*** The pharmaceutical supply chain can immensely benefit from better use of available data analytics, more effective monitoring and evaluation, and evidence-based decision-making. This can be supported by improved digitalization, including the scaling up use of the pharmaceutical IT system such as management dashboards and standardized Global Standards 1 (GS1) labelling, to improve the efficiency of the pharmaceutical supply chain.

(vii) ***Quality assurance.*** Premarketing quality assurance in Sri Lanka is mainly carried out at the time of product registration. Quality assurance during the procurement process is inadequate and lacks stringent quality checks, including routine prequalification at the manufacturer and importer levels. The point-of-entry quality control is inadequate and lacks physical infrastructure, capacity, and human resources to implement a comprehensive approach. Pharmacovigilance process and the practice are also at the nascent level. Quality tests are carried out mainly following the reporting of clinical quality failures and therefore, the high rate of quality test failures indicates the need for more proactive quality assurance mechanisms to prevent the possibility of substandard and falsified items entering the supply chain to continue public confidence in medicines available at the government health facilities.

(viii) ***Capacity building.*** Institutional training courses on pharmaceutical supply chains are not available in Sri Lanka and there is a lack of trained pharmaceutical supply chain professionals. Ensuring adequate human resources and orienting and refreshing professionals on pharmaceutical supply chain management would increase efficiency of the supply chain.

(ix) ***Market shaping.*** Current procurement practices lack market-shaping strategies and do not take advantage of framework agreements and other strategic procurement methods that encourage the markets to meet the requirements of the buyer. Strategic procurement practices, market shaping strategies, and use of framework agreements and pooled procurement mechanisms would reduce time, cost, and vulnerability of Sri Lanka's public health pharmaceutical supply chain to market volatility.

Recommendations. Based on global best practices, different models of supply chain including a more segmented and coordinated supply chain, using third party and fourth party logistics providers for direct delivery of health products to the health facilities, and using e-catalog and e-marketplace system are identified for Sri Lanka's consideration. For example, the role of MOH can be setting technical standards; conducting demand forecasting, prequalification, and price negotiation; formulating of framework agreements with the suppliers; setting quantity caps for end users; and setting up an e-marketplace system through that end users would be able to place and receive orders directly. Currently, Sri Lanka is practicing a centralized supply chain model led by MSD with a few vertical programs having their own segmented supply chain. Sri Lanka would benefit from incorporating key features of other models of supply chain.

Synthesizing the findings and analysis, the following pathways and recommended policy and program actions are identified for further improvement of and efficiency gains in Sri Lanka's public health-led pharmaceutical supply chain.

Pathway 1: Strengthen pharmaceutical supply chain governance

(i) Review and revise the organizational structure of current pharmaceutical governance systems to better streamline it for improving the efficiency of the pharmaceutical supply chain.

(ii) Optimize mechanisms used for product selection and rational use.

(iii) Review the pharmaceutical supply chain governance mechanism related to product selection and rational use.

(iv) Set up and/or strengthen necessary structures by clearly segregating the technical standards setting, policy making, regulatory, market shaping, procurement, logistics, and oversight roles. Implement adequate coordination and accountability.

(v) Set up units or enhance and empower technical committees within MOH for clinical excellence to take care of clinical standards, national treatment guidelines, national formulary, EML, and health technology assessments.

(vi) Update and streamline the practice of implementing and revising guidelines, including the EML and national treatment guidelines.

(vii) Implement the practice of generic prescription and prescription audits.

(viii) Develop an electronic tool for rational product selection.

(ix) Establish a National Institute of Clinical Excellence.

(x) Conduct periodic drug resistance monitoring surveys.

Pathway 2: Employ strategic procurement

(i) Use historical consumption data together with epidemiological and service delivery data for defining strategic procurement.

(ii) Develop policies and standard operating procedures for national forecasting and supply planning.

(iii) Integrate forecasting and supply planning modules within the currently practiced IT system (SWASTHA) and switch to new forecasting and supply planning practices.

(iv) Develop procurement strategies for different products (high and low value, high and low volume, shelf-life and half-life of the pharmaceutical etc.) and train relevant people to determine the most efficient and cost effective procurement methods and instruments.

(v) Introduce framework agreements.

(vi) Utilize an interoperable enterprise resource planning for procurement (epromise.lk).

(vii) Introduce prequalification, price negotiation, and e-catalog/e-market place where pre-qualified suppliers and products are listed with negotiated price for purchasers to place online order.

Pathway 3: Optimize storage and distribution network

(i) Undertake distribution network analysis and distribution system optimization exercises.

(ii) Address the storage condition issues in health facilities by allocating sufficient space, procuring sturdy shelves and pallets, and installing temperature and humidity monitors, smoke detectors, and air conditioners.

(iii) Set up more efficient inventory control and distribution policies.

(iv) Fill in vacant staff positions for pharmaceutical supply management.

(v) Train staff on inventory control, good storage, and distribution practice.

(vi) Redesign the distribution network based on options analysis.

Pathway 4: Improve data visibility and use data analytics

(i) Optimize the use of SWASTHA for electronic health records, electronic logistics management information system, forecasting, monitoring and evaluation, and early warnings.

(ii) Orient staff, managers, and decision makers on interpreting supply chain data and using supply chain data for decision-making.

(iii) Deploy and roll out information systems for NMRA, SPC, and MSD for product selection and specifications, product registration, procurement processing and management, e-catalog and e-procurement, quality assurance of medical products, and pharmacovigilance.

(iv) Develop a road map for implementing Global Standards 1 and barcode system.

(v) Strengthen the relevant committee within MOH for oversight, monitoring, and evaluation of the performance of pharmaceutical supply chain.

Pathway 5: Strengthen quality assurance and medicine regulatory system

(i) Strengthen NMRA and NMQAL by hiring and training the required number of staff.

(ii) Develop a road map for NMQAL to be an ISO certified and/or prequalified laboratory of the World Health Organization (WHO).

(iii) Implement a more comprehensive national quality assurance strategy including strengthening a risk-based point-of-entry testing mechanism.

(iv) Set up a national network of collaborative quality assurance laboratories with NMQAL taking the national reference laboratory and leadership role.

(v) Strengthen SPC's quality assurance laboratory.

(vi) Leverage WHO collaborative laboratory network.

(vii) Optimize product registration process, harmonize the common technical dossier (CTD) used by NMRA, and institutionalize accelerated and reliance pathways for product registration.

Pathway 6: Build pharmaceutical supply chain workforce capacity

(i) Orient key leaders, policy makers, and managers on pharmaceutical supply chain management.

(ii) Conduct a pharmaceutical supply chain workforce assessment and develop a workforce development plan.

(iii) Develop training courses and make preservice and in-service training arrangements for pharmaceutical supply chain workforce.

(iv) Implement pharmaceutical supply chain workforce development plan.

(v) Implement online training platform for in-service training on pharmaceutical supply chain.

(vi) Introduce pharmaceutical supply chain management courses in appropriate academic programs.

Pathway 7: Explore opportunities for setting up a regional mechanism for greater medicine access

(i) Conduct feasibility study for Sri Lanka to set up or take part in a regional and/or international quality assurance, market access, and pooled procurement mechanism.

(ii) Set up a commission or unit under MOH for employing price negotiation, market shaping, and pricing strategies.

(iii) Initiate setting up or taking part in a regional or international quality assurance, market access, and pooled procurement mechanism.

REPORT BACKGROUND

The purpose of this report is to understand the systemic vulnerabilities of the pharmaceutical supply chain and identify areas of further improvements to upgrade Sri Lanka's pharmaceutical supply chain to the next level of efficiency and effectiveness.

The data collection period for this assessment was not ideal, as it was marked by the COVID-19 pandemic back to back with an economic crisis affecting the pharmaceutical supply chain. Further, the pharmaceutical usage pattern was modified given the COVID-19 prevention and control efforts, and the required data was either not available or could not be verified against data from previous years. Nevertheless, the assessment tried to provide a high-level overview of Sri Lanka's pharmaceutical supply chain system, its organization, functions, strengths, and areas of improvement to increase its efficiency and reduce its vulnerabilities in the future.

Opinions expressed in this report are those of the assessment team and do not necessarily represent the opinions of the Asian Development Bank, development partners, Ministry of Health, Ministry of Finance, or Technical Working Group members who supported this assessment.

Chapter 1

INTRODUCTION

Sri Lanka has achieved commendable health outcomes compared to other countries of the same economic level. Sri Lanka has witnessed advancements in vital health measures; enhanced life expectancy; and eradication of diseases like malaria, measles, filariasis, polio, and neonatal tetanus. Nevertheless, the nation's health system needs to be upgraded to meet challenges from the changing economic, demographic, and epidemiological landscapes. The country needs more efficient health interventions to meet the demands of the aging population and increasing noncommunicable diseases, which currently contribute to around 75% of deaths.[1]

The public sector accounts for 95% of in-patient care and almost 100% of preventive care in Sri Lanka. Meanwhile, the private health care sector is growing and accounts for 50% of the out-patient care, and 5%–10% of inpatient care, which remains accessible only to a portion of the population due to high costs. The public sector curative service delivery reaches the population through 1,159 health facilities, out of which 59 larger Teaching and Specialized hospitals are administered by the central government, with approximately 50% of beds and more than two-thirds of specialist beds. Preventive health service is delivered through 356 preventive Medical Officer of Health areas, which are geographically defined areas with dedicated preventive health staff providing services to demarcated areas.

Sri Lanka provides all health services (preventive and primary, secondary, tertiary level curative care) free of charge to all citizens at point-of-delivery. In addition, the public sector employees have access to a social health insurance scheme (the Agrahara insurance scheme) for selected services. Other limited insurance schemes are also available for some large-scale private sector company employees.

With a per capita current health expenditure of $166.18, government health expenditure stands at around 4% of gross domestic product. Around 7% of the total budget is allocated to the health sector, and only about 4% of the total health expenditure by the government comes from external sources. However, around 44% of the current health expenditure comes from out-of-pocket expenses.[2] More than 30% of the annual health budget is spent on pharmaceuticals, which amounts to over $360 million of annual pharmaceutical procurement by the government.[3]

Sri Lanka's pharmaceutical supply chain is a mix of centrally managed and decentralized structures with procurement of pharmaceuticals managed at the central level. The key stakeholders in the current pharmaceutical governance systems include the Ministry of Health (MOH); National Medicines Regulatory Authority (NMRA) including the National Medicine Quality Assurance Laboratory (NMQAL), Medical Supplies Division (MSD), and 26 Regional Medical Supplies Divisions (RMSD); drug stores in each health care institution; State Pharmaceutical Corporation (SPC); State Pharmaceutical Manufacturing Corporation (SPMC); local medicine importers; and local manufacturers.

1 Government of Sri Lanka, Ministry of Health. 2020. *Annual Health Bulletin.*
2 World Health Organization (WHO). 2023. Regional Health Observatory—South East Asia. Updated 5 December 2023.
3 Sri Lanka Association of Clinical Pharmacology and Therapeutics. Evidence Synthesis on Essential Medicines Policy Reform Options for Sri Lanka. World Health Organization (Project No. 2022/1279296-0).

The NMRA is responsible for ensuring quality, safety, and efficacy of pharmaceutical products through product registration, quality assurance, and pharmacovigilance. As the national regulatory authority, NMRA exercises oversight on various regulatory functions including evaluation and registration of medicines for ensuring quality, safety, and efficacy, as well as for price regulation.[4] It is also the institutional home of the NMQAL, which is responsible for analyzing the quality of any medicine and medical devices. NMRA has a partnership with the University of Colombo to conduct pharmacovigilance activities.

Estimation, procurement initiation, storage, distribution, and monitoring of medical products fall under the purview of MSD in the MOH. The State Pharmaceutical Corporation serves as the procurement agent for MOH. Forecasting, distribution, and monitoring of supplies to the drug store of each health care institution are overseen by the MSD, in collaboration with 26 RMSDs based on an annual call for estimation of requirements from each health care facility in the country (Figure 1).

Figure 1: Flow of Commodities and Flow of Estimates

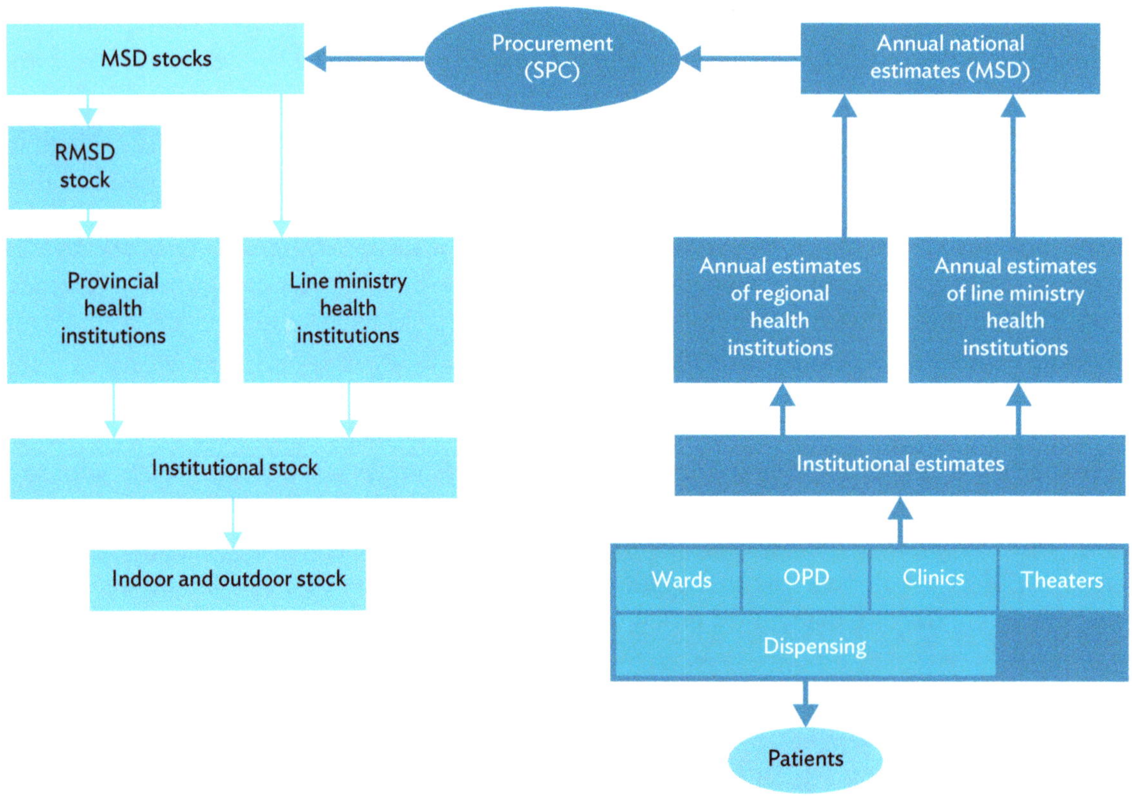

MSD = Medical Supplies Division, OPD = outpatient department, RMSD = Regional Medical Supplies Division, SPC = State Pharmaceutical Corporation.

Source: Government of Sri Lanka, Ministry of Health and Nutrition. 2008. *Manual on Management of Drugs. Second Revision.*

[4] Government of Sri Lanka. 2015. National Medicines Regulatory Authority Act.

In addition to estimating, storing, and distributing medical products, MSD also operates the Secretariat of the National Drug and Therapeutic Committee chaired by the Director General of Health Services. The National Drug and Therapeutic Committee creates the national procurement list for medicines and other supplies, currently also referred to as the priority list of pharmaceuticals, based on the Essential Medicines List (EML) albeit longer. Medicines that do not appear on the EML or priority list are at times included in the procurement list on the case-by-case requests by physicians and patient advocacy groups knowledgeable on new treatment modalities or their related aspects.

Once MSD has listed and quantified the medicines required by the health system, the list goes to SPC. Created in 1971, SPC is a semigovernment agency that is Sri Lanka's central purchaser and main supplier of pharmaceuticals, surgical consumable items, laboratory chemicals, and equipment to government health facilities. The functions of SPC include importation and purchase of medical products, contribution to retail pharmaceutical sales by operating 105 franchise pharmacies and 11 authorized retailers, and distributing to private retail pharmacies.

Over 180 private local pharmaceutical establishments are currently registered as NMRA importers. These include local conglomerates that act as local representatives distributing medicines from multinational companies as well as wholesalers and distributors for smaller regional manufacturers.

In Sri Lanka, 16.4% of the pharmaceutical market is captured by local manufacturers including the SPMC.[5] The SPMC is the largest state-owned drug manufacturer in Sri Lanka, providing 43 medicines to the MOH. Currently, 20 manufacturers approved by the NMRA are in operation and about 5 new facilities are being commissioned.

The publicly available EML was revised in 2013–2014 and then in 2021.[6] MSD made a formulary revision and published an approved list of pharmaceutical items in 2016–2017, which was updated in 2019. The formulary revision in 2019 included a total of 1,346 medicines categorized as vital (14 items), essential (675 items), and nonessential (657 items) in their different dosage forms for purchase for the public sector. The EML itself has 383 medicines that include 675 items in different dosage forms. The most recent revision of the list of medicines for the hospitals was made in February–April 2023, chaired by the director general of Health Services with representatives of specialty colleges and associations. The 2023 revision identified a priority list of 850 items including 643 normal stock items, 21 raw materials, 10 antidotes, 77 items for special campaigns, 2 miscellaneous items, and 97 items to be supplied on a named patient basis.[7]

From previous studies and reports, it appears that irrational use of medicines is prevalent in the country including polypharmacy, irrational use of antimicrobials, and self-medication.[8]

5 Sri Lanka Chamber of Pharmaceutical Industry. 2019. *The Future of Pharmaceutical Manufacturing in Sri Lanka*.
6 Government of Sri Lanka. Medical Supply Division. Ministry of Health.
7 Government of Sri Lanka. 2024. *MOH Circular No. 01/14-2023. 4 April (Internal)*. Ministry of Health.
8 G. P. Senadheera et al. 2017. Practice of Self-Medication with Antibiotics in the Colombo District, Sri Lanka. *Ceylon Med J.* 62 (1).pp. 70–72.

Recent reports—including two reports by Sri Lanka Association of Clinical Pharmacology and Therapeutics,[9] the Special Report by the Auditor General,[10] and the Report of the Public Expenditure Review Committee[11]—have reiterated pressing challenges including lengthy product registration system, suboptimal forecasting process, long procurement lead time, absence of efficient information systems, frequent stockouts of health commodities, staff shortage, and weak technical capacities faced by the pharmaceutical supply chain system in Sri Lanka.

Against this backdrop, the MOH—together with the Ministry of Finance of Sri Lanka with support from ADB and other development partners—undertook this assessment to examine the status, bottlenecks, and opportunities for improvement at all levels of the public health supply chain management in Sri Lanka and identify actionable options for the government for graduating to a more efficient and resilient pharmaceutical supply chain.

9 Sri Lanka Association of Clinical Pharmacology and Therapeutics. Evidence Synthesis on Essential Medicines Policy Reform Options for Sri Lanka. World Health Organization (Project No. 2022/1279296-0); Sri Lanka Association of Clinical Pharmacology and Therapeutics. 2023. Challenges and Barriers for Effective Supply of Medicines to the State Sector and Recommendations to the Ministry of Health Sri Lanka.

10 Government of Sri Lanka, Office of the Auditor General. 2022. *Auditor General's Special Report on Procedures Taken to Avoid the Shortage of Pharmaceuticals in Government Hospitals by 13 May 2022.*

11 Government of Sri Lanka, Public Expenditure Review Committee. 2023. Report of the Public Expenditure Review Committee on Rationalization of Government Expenditure Relating to the Ministry of Health.

Chapter 2

OBJECTIVES

The specific objectives of the assessment are as follows:

(i) Generate an overall understanding of the current organization and functioning of the public health pharmaceutical supply chain in Sri Lanka.

(ii) Diagnose the key barriers and identify the factors affecting the efficiency and effectiveness of the pharmaceutical supply chain.

(iii) Analyze well-informed options for addressing the identified gaps and develop models for enhancing the capability and performance of the pharmaceutical supply chain by drawing insights from appropriate good and promising practices.

(iv) Outline specific areas requiring future investments to strengthen the supply chain in Sri Lanka's health sector, while optimizing resource allocation.

Chapter 3

CONCEPTUAL FRAMEWORK

For the assessment, an ecosystem-based pharmaceutical systems strengthening approach was employed. Pharmaceutical systems strengthening is defined as "The process of identifying and implementing strategies and actions that achieve coordinated and sustainable improvements in the critical components of a pharmaceutical system to make it more responsive and resilient and to enhance its performance for achieving better health outcomes."[12]

As presented in Figure 2, the pharmaceutical supply chain consists of all structures, people, resources, processes, and their interactions within the broader health system and market ecosystem to ensure equitable and timely access to safe, effective, and quality-assured pharmaceutical products and related services and promote their appropriate and cost-effective use to improve health outcomes.

Figure 2: Pharmaceutical Supply Chain Assessment Framework

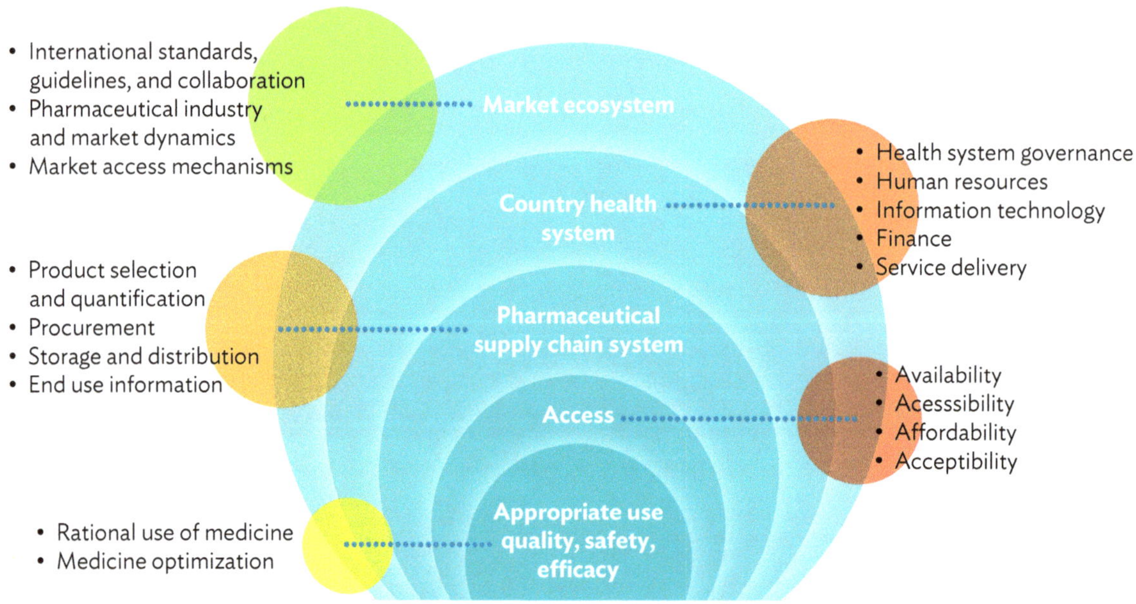

Source: Asian Development Bank assessment team.

12 M. Soucy Brown et al. 2021. *PSS Insight v2.0—A Framework and Indicators for Measuring Pharmaceutical Systems Strengthening*. p. 13.

The assessment investigated the following conceptual areas for a comprehensive review of Sri Lanka's pharmaceutical supply chain:

(i) Systems in place for ensuring quality, safety, and efficacy of medical products.

(ii) Appropriate use of medical products including rational use of medicines and medicine optimizations.

(iii) Access to medical products including availability, service delivery, accessibility, finance, affordability, and acceptability.

(iv) Pharmaceutical supply chain system including
  (a) product selection,
  (b) quantification,
  (c) procurement,
  (d) warehousing,
  (e) transportation and distribution,
  (f) end use information including digital information systems,
  (g) waste disposal, and
  (h) drug resistance monitoring.

(v) Enabling factors including governance (policy and regulatory framework) and human resources.

(vi) Market ecosystem including pharmaceutical industry and market dynamics, international collaboration, and market access mechanisms.

A list of 25 performance indicators drawn from the National Supply Chain Assessment 2.0.2 Toolkit[13] and Pharmaceutical System Strengthening Insight[14] were selected to assess key aspects of this framework. The indicators are presented in Table 1.

Table 1: Selected Performance Indicators for the Pharmaceutical Supply Chain Assessment Framework

Area	Indicator
Appropriate use of medicines	Percentage availability of National Treatment Guidelines that have been reviewed or updated within the last 3 years
Appropriate use of medicines	Percentage of medicines prescribed according to National Treatment Guidelines
Quality	Percentage of samples received by the National Medicine Quality Assurance Laboratory that failed quality control testing
Safety: Pharmacovigilance	Percentage of recorded adverse event reports that were assessed for causality
Efficacy	Presence of an Essential Medicine List (EML)

continued on next page

13 United States Agency for International Development. 2023. *Global Health Supply Chain Program. NSCA 2.0.2 Took Kit.*
14 M. Soucy Brown et al. 2021. *PSS Insight v2.0—A Framework and Indicators for Measuring Pharmaceutical Systems Strengthening.*

Table 1 *continued*

Area	Indicator
Availability	Proportion of health facilities that have a core set of relevant essential medicines (according to the National Formulary) available and affordable on a sustainable basis
Availability	Percentage of product losses by value due to expired medicines or damage or theft per value received
Service delivery and accessibility	Average distance of households from a dispensing facility or pharmacy
Finance and affordability	Out-of-pocket expenditure on pharmaceuticals out of total out-of-pocket expenditure for health
Acceptability	Percentage of patients surveyed satisfied with pharmaceutical services from their last visit to a public health facility
Product selection	Percentage of medicines selected from EML over the total number of medicines procured
Forecasting and supply planning	Mean percentage of variation between the forecast and actual consumption for a set of tracer products
Procurement	Percentage of median international price paid for a set of tracer medicines that was part of the last procurement
Procurement	Percentage of supplier with on-time and in full delivery (disaggregated by three types of procurement: regular procurement, local procurement, and emergency procurement)
Warehouse and distribution	Percentage of key storage conditions satisfied
Warehouse and distribution	Percentage of orders received on-time and in-full
Warehouse and distribution	Percentage of temperature-controlled vehicles in the total distribution fleet
End use: Logistics Management Information System (LMIS)	Percentage of health facilities that submit complete LMIS reports on time to their reporting unit
Information system	Data on safety, efficacy, and cost effectiveness of medicines available and used to inform essential medicines selection
End use: Drug resistance monitoring	Percentage of key action items implemented from the National Action Plan on Antimicrobial Resistance
End use: Waste disposal	Percentage of pharmaceutical wastes disposed according to the appropriate guidelines
Governance, policies, and regulatory framework	• Existence of a policy or strategy that sets standards for collection and management of pharmaceutical supply chain information for monitoring and evaluation • Index to assess the relevance and appropriateness of the current pharmaceutical procurement guidelines in meeting the specific needs and challenges of the health care system • Average number of days for decision making on a medicine application for registration
Human resources	Proportion of pharmaceutical supply chain positions that are filled in with licensed pharmacists, pharmacy technicians, or pharmacy assistants
Market ecosystem	Percentage of products on EML that are currently manufactured or comanufactured within the country

Source: Asian Development Bank assessment team.

Chapter 4

METHODOLOGY

The assessment was guided by a technical working group (TWG) comprising experts from relevant government units, development partners, and representatives from industry and professional associations in Sri Lanka. The assessment was facilitated and supported by an assessment team (an international expert in pharmaceutical supply chain as principal investigator, and a local consultant as co-investigator) mobilized by ADB, with participation from the World Health Organization (WHO) and United Nations Children's Fund (UNICEF).

The team carried out the assessment from August 2023 to May 2024 and employed multiple methods to achieve objectives: desk reviews, evaluation of facilities based on stratified random sampling across the whole country, patient satisfaction surveys, key informant interviews, focus group discussions, and a national consultation workshop. Details of the comprehensive methodology, questionnaires, and data set are provided in Appendix 1.

4.1 Data Collection

The study followed a mixed methods approach comprising both qualitative and quantitative data collection methods.

(i) **Desk review.** Review of policy documents, operational guidelines, administrative records, and historical data was done by the principal investigator.

(ii) **Facilities assessment.** An island-wide descriptive cross-section assessment was done selecting a sample of 79 health facilities. The sample size was calculated using a standard formula for a stratified random sampling. The desired number of facilities were selected from each stratum randomly as indicated in Table 2.

Table 2: Sample Sizes for Facilities Assessment

Type of Facility	Total Number of Facilities	Facilities Selected
Tertiary care facility	51	7
Base hospital A	36	7
Base hospital B	45	3
District hospital A	66	10
District hospital B	147	12
District hospital C	272	17
Primary medical care unit	542	23
Total	**1,159**	**79**

Sources: Ministry of Health and Asian Development Bank assessment team.

A pretested questionnaire was administered by two trained data collectors who visited all the selected facilities and filled in the questionnaire through interviews and observations.

Additionally, the assessment team visited 12 facilities including MSD and RMSD, as well as facilities from different levels—national hospitals, provincial hospitals, teaching hospitals, base hospitals, district hospitals, and primary medical care units—in three provinces (western, central, and southern) for facilities assessment, insights gathering, and onsite verification.

(iii) **Patient satisfaction survey.** A sample of patients (110) selected from different levels of health facilities were assessed for their satisfaction on service using an interviewer-administered questionnaire. Three trained data collectors were employed for this task.

(iv) **Key informant interviews.** A series of in-depth interviews with key stakeholders, including health officials, supply chain managers, health care practitioners, and industry representatives were conducted by the principal investigator and co-investigator to gather insights and information on the participant's area of knowledge and experience. A structured interviewer guide was utilized to direct the conversation. Saturation point was reached after interviewing eight respondents.

(v) **Focus group discussions.** The principal investigator and co-investigator conducted five focus group discussions (FGDs) with the private sector, MSD, SPC, NMRA, and Health Informatics Team of MOH to gather perspectives on challenges, root causes, opportunities for improvement, and policy recommendations.

(vi) **National consultative workshop.** The TWG organized a 2-day national consultative workshop on 24–25 November 2023 in Colombo with the participation of all levels of stakeholders involved in the pharmaceutical supply chain in Sri Lanka. The workshop provided the opportunity to engage in discussions and to build consensus on priority issues and preferred options.

4.2 Data Analysis

Data collected from the qualitative and quantitative methodologies were analyzed thematically by the principal investigator with assistance from the team of experts assigned by ADB, WHO, and UNICEF. Quantitative data collected from the facilities surveys and patient satisfaction surveys were analyzed using Microsoft Excel.

Final results of data analysis were grouped and presented according to the areas of the conceptual framework that cut across the entire pharmaceutical supply chain of Sri Lanka.

4.3 Presentation and Review of Findings

Key findings and policy options from the report were further presented to and reviewed by the TWG on 27 May 2024 and at a high-level stakeholder meeting convened by the Ministry of Health on 6 June 2024.

Chapter 5

FINDINGS

5.1 Systems for Ensuring Quality, Safety, and Efficacy

According to the Sri Lanka Procurement Guidelines 2022, quality, safety, and efficacy are ensured in the pharmaceutical supply chain upon authorization of quality tests at each of the following points (see also Figure 3):[15]

(i) preshipment inspection in exporting countries;

(ii) prepurchase testing of samples supplied by suppliers. However, significantly the Guidelines states that: "...samples may not be representative of the product that will be actually sold or delivered" and hence recommends: "... analysis of individual batches either by itself or through international quality control organizations/laboratories in order to ensure that the product to be sourced meet with the stipulated criteria."

Figure 3: Current System for Ensuring Quality, Safety, and Efficacy

Sources: Ministry of Health and Asian Development Bank assessment team.

[15] See Quality Assurance on pages 42 and 43 in Government of Sri Lanka. 2022. *Guidelines for Procurement of Pharmaceutical and Medical Devices of a Consumable Nature* (accessed March 2023).

(iii) laboratory testing of random batch samples, mandatory for new suppliers and manufacturers;

(iv) microbiological tests and pharmacological tests for selected pharmaceutical products;

(v) prepurchase and/or preshipment testing by an independent or WHO-recognized laboratory; and

(vi) postshipment laboratory testing of random batch samples and locally sourced products.

5.1.1 Quality

Quality assurance refers to systems for monitoring and taking action to ensure that pharmaceutical products in the distribution system meet specified quality standards; and for detecting, evaluating, and preventing product-related quality problems.

The National Medicines Regulatory Authority was established as the responsible authority to conduct postmarketing surveillance on quality, safety, and adverse reaction to the medicines; on medical devices; and on oversight of import (see footnote 4). At present, quality assurance is mostly limited to analyzing test samples of medicines provided by suppliers at the time of applying for registration. A limited practice of testing of random samples taken from the market for postregistration testing has also been observed. However, due to limited capacity and human resources, NMRA cannot fully perform a more proactive and premarketing quality assurance role to prevent substandard and falsified medical products from entering the supply chain. Concerns have emerged that the quality assurance gap may create the possibility of entry of substandard and falsified medicines to the market, which in the longer term may erode public confidence in the quality of medicines, especially those dispensed through the public health care institutions.

As mentioned, NMQAL conducts limited postmarketing quality tests for mostly the products submitted for registration and products with complaints. Table 3 presents the quality assurance-related decisions made by NMRA from 2021 to 2023.

Table 3: Quality Decisions by the National Medicines Regulatory Authority, 2021–2023

	2021	2022	2023
Batch or product withdrawn	42	44	60
Batch or product withheld	20	28	34
Revoked	22	10	0
Discontinued	1	4	1
Total	**85**	**86**	**95**

Source: National Medicines Regulatory Authority.

The NMRA particularly the NMQAL have been suffering from severe staff shortages. The NMRA reported that it would require over 500 staff to be able to perform its role comprehensively and at full capacity. However, the current total number of cadres for NMRA approved by the Department of Management Services is 269. Against these requirements, NMRA currently has only 127 existing cadre including 112 permanent cadre and 15 MOH employees.[16]

The NMQAL is particularly hardest-hit and has been running at 25% required staff positions (only 11 staff are currently available) as no staff recruitment has taken place since 2015. The laboratory facilities of NMQAL need to be upgraded and the building needs to be renovated to support testing activities that meet aspects of good laboratory practices as well as quality assurance of test results. The staff competency needs to be strengthened to assure the quality of the testing results. Also, NMQAL needs to be ISO-certified and prequalified by WHO to gain recognition as a national testing control laboratory.

(i) **Premarketing quality assurance.** At present, premarketing quality assurance in Sri Lanka mostly relies on the certificate of product registration with NMRA and licensing of manufacturing facilities. Ensuring product quality during procurement was not carried out or was compromised in some cases of emergency procurement especially in 2022/2023. As the procurement agent of the MOH, SPC is also not conducting prequalification at the manufacturer level for all its procurement, and point-of-entry quality check is not adequately practiced. It has been reported that quality issues in some medicines were not detected until after most of the batch had already been distributed and even used.

(ii) **Quality assurance of donated products.** Another area of quality concern is that during the economic crisis period, medicines received through donations from other countries and private organizations or individuals were supplied to hospitals without the required regulatory oversight and quality assurance. In some instances, product labeling regulations had been violated, where the labeling had been in a different language, making it very difficult for doctors and nurses to identify and confirm the medicine being administered to patients. In some cases, stocks of expired or short-expiry medicines, those that were not needed, and inappropriate dosage forms were received as donations.[17]

Although there are medicines donation guidelines developed by the WHO[18] and adopted in Sri Lanka for pharmaceutical donations, it seems these guidelines were not followed in receiving many donated medicines during the economic crisis period.

[16] Government of Sri Lanka, Department of Management Services. 2024. Quarterly Cadre Information Sheet. 5 June.
[17] Sri Lanka Association of Clinical Pharmacology and Therapeutics. Evidence Synthesis on Essential Medicines Policy Reform Options for Sri Lanka. World Health Organization (Project No. 2022/1279296-0).
[18] WHO. 2011. *Guidelines for Medicine Donations Revised 2010* (accessed January 2024).

5.1.2 Safety

Safety focuses on minimizing the risks associated with the use of medicines and involves a system for detecting, evaluating, and preventing drug-related adverse reactions known as pharmacovigilance. According to a WHO Global Benchmarking Assessment (2019),[19] NMRA has an organization chart that includes the Pharmacovigilance Division with allocated human resources but the roles and responsibilities of the staff members responsible for pharmacovigilance are not appropriately defined. A general SOP for pharmacovigilance exists; however, not all processes are described. The Quality Management System is not well implemented for pharmacovigilance, although the NMRA has initiated the Quality Management System in other functions. The staff development and training plans are in the development stage and a communication plan needs to be developed.

As seen in Table 4, pharmacovigilance reporting was extremely low in 2021 and 2022. In 2023, the reporting numbers improved due to an effort by NMRA to promote pharmacovigilance reporting including reporting via electronic means. A total of 300 adverse events out of the total 335 reports were analyzed for causality in 2023.

Table 4: Pharmacovigilance Reports Received and Analyzed by the National Medicines Regulatory Authority

Period	No. of Reports Received	No. of Reports Analyzed	Percentage of Analysis
January–December 2021	31	31	100
January–December 2022	13	13	100
January–October 2023	335	300	90

Source: National Medicines Regulatory Authority.

The current practice related to pharmacovigilance is based on spontaneous reporting of adverse events by the treatment providers. The challenge with a spontaneous reporting system is low reporting and lack of a denominator to analyze the reports and detect the “signals” needing required actions. There is no targeted spontaneous or active surveillance system in place for pharmacovigilance of new and high-risk medicines.

In February 2024, the country took the initiative to report to the WHO Programme for International Drug Monitoring (Uppsala Monitoring Centre) for Pharmacovigilance. As of March 2024, the country was not using any digital information system for reporting and analyzing adverse drug reactions and adverse events except an adverse event following immunization (AEFI) database for vaccines managed by the Epidemiology Unit.[20]

19 Source: WHO. 2019. Benchmarking of the National Regulatory Authority (NRA) GBT. Rev VI, ver. 1. Sri Lanka.

20 Government of Sri Lanka, Ministry of Health. 2012. *National Guidelines on Immunization Safety Surveillance: Surveillance of Adverse Effects Following Immunization*.

5.1.3 Efficacy

Efficacy indicates the ability of a medicine to produce the desired therapeutic effect under specific conditions. While NMRA considers quality, safety, and efficacy of a medicine during registration, countries maintain an EML based on efficacy and cost-effectiveness to limit the variations in prescribing and product selection within the same therapeutic group.

Although Sri Lanka has an EML that was introduced by MOH, there is no health technology assessment unit to support evaluation of efficacy and cost-effectiveness of medicines listed in the Essential Medicine List. There is no dedicated technical unit to take care of the EML apart from MSD hosting the secretariat of an EML technical committee.

In Sri Lanka, the national procurement list of medicinal products is developed by the National Drugs and Therapeutics Committee composed of relevant experts as well as the Director General of Health Services. However, there are no standardized terms of reference for the National Drug Therapeutic Committee to implement national medicine policies. It was reported that decisions pertaining to the requirement of medicines were often taken by the Formulary Revision Committee through the National Procurement List. This missed the opportunity for a detailed assessment of therapeutic efficacy and cost-effectiveness of medicines by relevant experts before a medicine was included in the national procurement list.

5.2 Appropriate Use of Medical Products

Appropriate use of medical products refers to the judicious and responsible utilization of safe, high-quality, and efficacious medications and other medical products in a manner that aligns with established clinical guidelines and patient-specific considerations. Service providers prescribing medicines are expected to follow rational prescribing, use generic names and standard treatment guidelines to avoid poly pharmacy, brand preference, and overprescribing.

A desk review on the availability of national treatment guidelines that have been reviewed or updated within the past three years or since 2021 finds the guidelines to be limited (Table 5). Implementation of the national treatment guidelines is not being monitored in a systematic manner. Likewise, development of these guidelines is ad hoc and there is no dedicated unit or institute taking care of treatment standards.

Currently, there is no systematic mechanism to promote or monitor the rational use of medicines. There are no prescription audits carried out and rational prescribing is not always practiced due to poor training and limited awareness on national treatment guidelines. In the absence of strict implementation of national treatment guidelines, prescribing patterns differ among specialists even in the same field, generating the need for a wide variety of medical products to be procured.

Table 5: Last Update Dates of Some Sample National Treatment Guidelines

National Treatment Guideline	Updating Entity	Last Updated
Guidelines on Management of Dengue Fever and Dengue Hemorrhagic Fever in Children and Adolescents	Sri Lanka College of Pediatricians	2012
Diabetes Mellitus Management Guidelines	Sri Lanka College of Endocrinologists	2018
The Guideline Use of Antiretroviral Drugs for Treating and Prevention of HIV Infection	National STD AIDS Control Programme, Ministry of Health, Sri Lanka	2014
National Guideline For Management of Hypertension For Secondary and Tertiary Health Care Level	Directorate of Non-Communicable Diseases, Ministry of Health	2021

Source: From a review of National Treatment Guidelines.

Box 1 summarizes the quality, safety, and efficacy issues besetting the pharmaceutical supply chain in Sri Lanka.

Box 1: Key Gaps Identified in Quality, Safety, Efficacy, and Appropriate Use

- Need for an institutionalized regular mechanism to review, revise, and approve clinical standards and national treatment guidelines.
- Quality assurance activity could be more comprehensive in addition to testing samples for product registration and samples with complaints.
- Post marketing surveillance does not test adequate number of samples due to the capacity constraint of National Medicines Regulatory Authority and National Medicine Quality Assurance Laboratory.
- Inadequate pre-marketing quality assurance mechanism hinders the prevention of substandard and falsified medical products entering the supply chain
- The National Medicines Regulatory Authority and National Medicine Quality Assurance Laboratory cannot function optimally due to shortage of trained staff.
- No digital information system is used for collecting, storing, and analyzing pharmacovigilance reports.
- Rational prescribing based on the principles of limiting prescription variations, selecting products based on therapeutic efficacy and cost-effectiveness, and ensuring rational use of medicines are not adequately practiced.

Source: Asian Development Bank assessment team.

5.3 Access

Access comprises availability, accessibility, affordability, and acceptability (Figure 4).

Figure 4: Current Ministry of Health System for Ensuring the Access of Pharmaceuticals

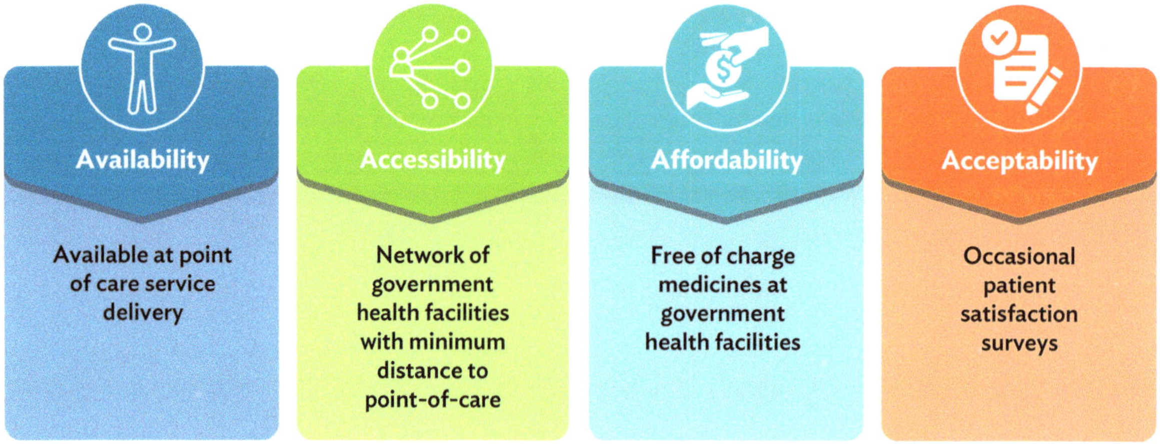

Sources: Ministry of Health and Asian Development Bank assessment team.

5.3.1 Availability

Availability involves the consistent presence of quality-assured medicines and other medical products in health care settings, ensuring a stable supply to meet the demand.

Out of the 108 patients who responded during the patient satisfaction surveys conducted from September to November 2023, 45.4% reported nonavailability of one or more prescribed medicines at the health facility. For the health facilities assessed during the same period, in response to the question if all essential medicines (according to National Formulary Revision 2019) were available at the health facility, only 11.5% of total 78 responses said yes (Figure 5).

Figure 5: Availability of Medicines at Point of Care as Reported by Patients and Facilities, 2023

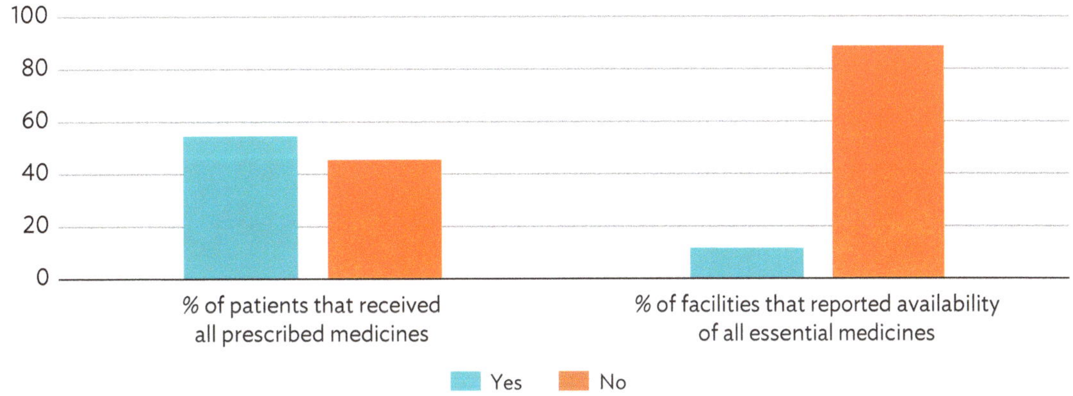

Note: Data collected through the facilities assessment questionnaire and patient satisfaction surveys.

In contrast to these findings, previous studies on the availability of essential medicines in Sri Lanka, in general, showed good availability and access to medicines.[21]

While there were pervasive product availability issues, there were still some issues related to products expiring on the shelf without being consumed.

Table 6 presents an analysis of data on product expiry cases captured from the medical supply management information system (MSMIS) used prior to June 2023 and the new system, *Swastha* is a Sanskrit word meaning "health and well-being." launched from June 2023.[22] Results show that the total value of reported health commodity loss due to expiry in the 12 months period starting from 1 November 2022 to 31 October 2023 was 4,064,170,083 Sri Lankan rupees (SLR) or around $12,418,401.[23] However, more than two-thirds value of this expiry was related to COVID-19 commodities, which had a short shelf life.

---

[21] B. M. R. Fernandopulle et al. Patient Experiences of Access to NCD Medicines in Sri Lanka: Evidence of the Success Story Towards Universal Coverage. *Medicine Access @ Point of Care*; WHO. 2015. Medicines in Health Care Delivery: Sri Lanka Situational Analysis.

[22] MSMIS-SWASTHA is an integrated electronic health records and logistics management information system introduced in 2023 to replace the MSMIS (Pronto). MSMIS (Pronto) was introduced in 2015 to link MSD with SPC, RMSDs, hospitals, and selected provincial hospitals.

[23] $1 = SLR327.27 as of 30 October 2023 (source: poundsterlinglive).

Table 6: Value of Health Commodity Loss Due to Expiry, November 2022–October 2023

Category	Item	% Expired	Value of Expired Lots (SLR)	Value of Expired Lots ($)
COVID-19	COVID-19 Vaccines	68.9	2,800,363,835	8,556,739
COVID-19	COVID-19 Tests	3.4	137,860,046	421,243
	Value of Total COVID-19 Products Expired	**72.3**	**2,938,223,881**	**8,977,981**
Non-COVID-19	Expired at RMSD	1.3	52,937,940	161,756
	Expired at Other Facilities	26.4	1,073,008,262	3,278,664
	Value of Total Non-COVID-19 Products Expired	**27.7**	**1,125,946,202**	**3,440,420**
Total Value of Expired Products		**100%**	**4,064,170,083**	**12,418,401**

COVID-19 = coronavirus disease, MSMIS = Medical Supply Management Information System, RMSD = regional medical supply division, SLR = Sri Lankan rupee.
Note: $1 = SLR327.27 as of 30 October 2023 (source: poundsterlinglive).
Source: Analysis of data from SWASTHA and MSMIS (Pronto).

Table 7 provides further analyses of percentage of stock value lost due to product expiry excluding COVID-19 items.

Table 7: Percentage of Product Value Lost (excluding COVID-19 items) Due to Expiry, November 2022–October 2023

Place of Expiry	Value of Total Stock (SLR)	Value of Total Stock ($)	Total Value of Expired Items (SLR)	Total Value of Expired Items ($)	Portion of Expired Value (%)
MSD	14,597,544,169	44,603,979	0	0	0.0
Facilities	17,458,538,467	53,345,979	1,125,946,202	3,440,420	6.4
Total	**32,056,082,636**	**97,949,958**	**1,125,946,202**	**3,440,420**	**3.5**

COVID-19 = coronavirus disease, MSD = Medical Supply Division, MSMIS = Medical Supply Management Information System, SLR = Sri Lankan rupee.
Note: $1 = SLR327.27 as of 30 October 2023 (source: poundsterlinglive).
Source: Analysis of data from SWASTHA and MSMIS (Pronto).

Among non-COVID-19 expired items, the five top value items that expired at facilities were Hemofiltration Solution 5-liter bag for continuous renal replacement therapy machines, Metaraminol injection 10 milligram (mg) in 1 milliliter (ml) ampoule, Flumazenil injection 500 microgram (mcg) in 5 ml vial/ampoule, strips for cholesterol meter, and nucleic acid extraction kits. On the other hand, the top five high-value items that expired at the RMSD level were Cefuroxime Sodium injection 250 mg vial, Dried Factor VIII fraction 200IU-350IU vial, strips for cholesterol meter, sodium chloride for IV use 0.9%, and Flumazenil injection 500 mcg in 5 ml vial/ampoule.

It is noted that no items expired at the MSD level as MSD usually transfers items that are close to expiry to RMSD and health facilities. However, the percentage of stock value lost due to the items expired at the drug stores of the health care facilities was 6.4% of the total stock value at the facilities. While product expiry during the COVID-19 pandemic was exceptional, expiry of non-COVID-19 items indicates potential issues related to product selection, minimum stock requirement for procurement, inaccurate forecasting, overstocking, stock imbalance, and poor management of stocks.

5.3.2 Service Delivery and Accessibility

Accessibility encompasses the ease with which individuals can obtain medicines and pharmaceutical services. Accessibility is closely linked with the service delivery system through the organization of interconnected facilities, transport, processes, and information flows to ensure the cost-effective and efficient delivery of products or services where they are needed. Sri Lanka has set up an excellent health service delivery network for curative and preventive services with a total 1,159 health facilities and 354 MOH areas across the country (Table 8).

Table 8: Number of Health Facilities in Sri Lanka, 2020

Level of Care	Health Facility Type	Number of Hospitals		
		Line Ministry	Provincial Ministry	Total
Tertiary Care	National hospital	2	0	2
	Teaching hospital	10	0	10
	Specialized teaching hospital	6	0	6
	Other specialized hospital	8	4	12
	Provincial general hospital	2	0	2
	District general hospital	13	6	19
Secondary Care	Base hospital Type A	6	30	36
	Base hospital Type B	1	44	45
Primary Care	Divisional hospital Type A	1	65	66
	Divisional hospital Type B	1	146	147
	Divisional hospital Type C	1	271	272
	Primary medical care unit	8	534	542
	TOTAL	**59**	**1,100**	**1,159**

Source: Government of Sri Lanka, Ministry of Health. 2020. *Annual Health Bulletin 2020*.

This network has brought the government health services within a 5-kilometer average proximity to the population.[24]

[24] L. Rajapaksa et al. 2021. *Sri Lanka Health System Review*. World Health Organization Regional Office for South-East Asia.

5.3.3 Affordability and Finance

Affordability is ensuring that the cost of medicines is reasonable and within financial reach for individuals and health systems irrespective of their economic standing. The Government of Sri Lanka is committed to offer free health services and medications to its people. Thus, all prescribed medicines are offered free of charge at the point-of-care of the government health facilities, making access to medicines very affordable to Sri Lankans.

Sri Lanka's health system is designed in such a way to make sure that health care users receive required medicines free of charge through the public procurement system. Yet 34% of out-of-pocket expenditures for health are spent for pharmaceuticals.[25] Possible reasons for out-of-pocket expenditures for pharmaceuticals include preference for obtaining services in the private sector, lack of availability of prescribed medicines at the government facility, brand preference among patients and medical professionals, and high pharmaceutical costs at the private facilities.

According to the National Health Accounts, the Sri Lankan government allocates $8 per capita for the procurement of pharmaceuticals.[26] Figure 6 presents the annual revised budget for pharmaceutical procurement segregated by disbursement entities, i.e., SPC, SPMC, MSD, and hospitals.

Historically, all pharmaceutical procurements were 100% covered by domestic sources in Sri Lanka although with issues related to lack of timely payment to all suppliers. However, the economic crisis and the resulting shortage of foreign currency in 2021 and 2022 led to major gaps in the flow of funds for ordering the pharmaceuticals. As a direct result, the pharmaceutical supply chain was severely

Figure 6: Annual Pharmaceutical Procurement Budget, 2020–2023
(SLR billion)

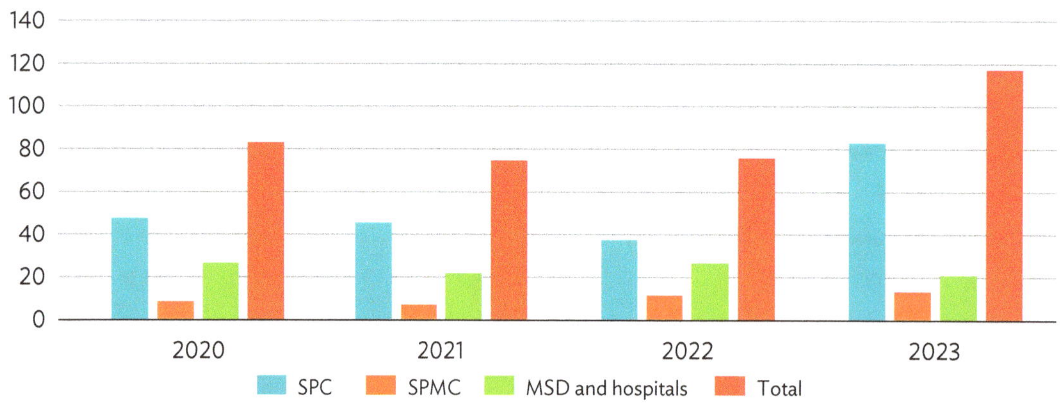

MSD = Medical Supplies Division, SPC = State Pharmaceutical Corporation, SPMC = State Pharmaceutical Manufacturing Corporation, SLR = Sri Lankan rupee.
Source: Ministry of Health.

25 WHO. 2023. *Access to Medical Products in the South-East Asia Region*.

26 Government of Sri Lanka, Ministry of Health. 2022. *National Health Accounts Sri Lanka 2017 & 2018*. Human Resource Management Coordinating Unit.

affected, as availability of foreign currency was not predictable during this period. The country had to postpone and cancel many procurements and there was a significant backlog payment to be cleared. According to the Auditor General's Special Report, the total amount payable to suppliers and banks by 20 April 2022 for medical supplies ordered by SPC from the local market was around SLR4.3 billion (approximately US$15 million) and the MOH owed around SLR35 billion (approximately US$115 million) to SPC until 2023.[27]

Further, to address the "emergency" situation of nonavailability of pharmaceuticals, emergency procurement procedures were utilized using the donor-financed funds that were made available from 2022 onward. By 2023, an unprecedented 46.6% of the pharmaceutical procurement budget came from foreign sources.

5.3.4 Acceptability

Acceptability refers to acknowledging cultural, social, and patient-specific factors that may influence the willingness of individuals to accept and adhere to prescribed medicines. Even though 45.4% of patients interviewed mentioned lack of one or more prescribed medicines at the health facility they visited, thanks to convenient access and free health service, 74% patients expressed high satisfaction and 14% expressed moderate satisfaction with the pharmaceutical services they received.

Figure 7 shows the results of patient satisfaction from 108 responses when patients were asked "On a scale of 1 to 10, how satisfied are you with the overall pharmaceutical services you received at this health facility? (1 being very dissatisfied and 10 being very satisfied)."

Figure 7: Patient Satisfaction with Pharmaceutical Services
(N=108)

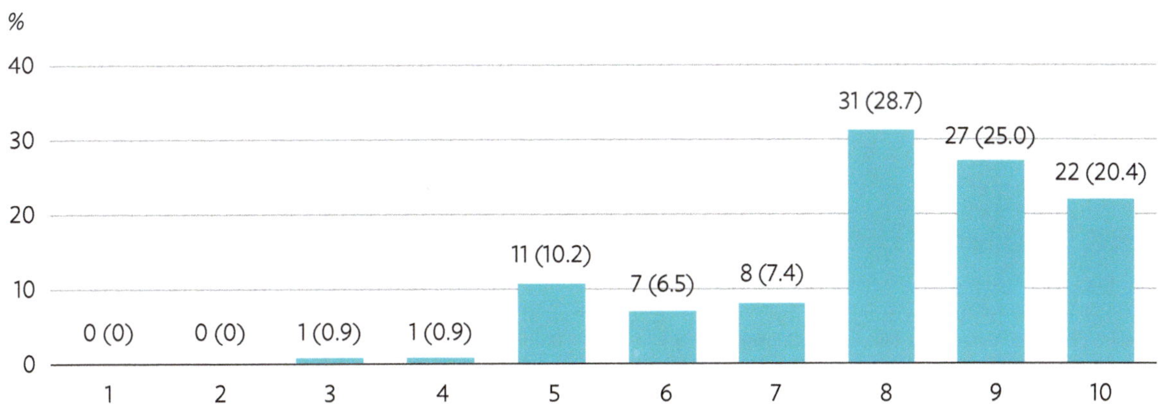

Note: 1 = very dissatisfied and 10 = very satisfied.
Source: Data collected through the patient satisfaction surveys.

[27] Government of Sri Lanka, Office of the Auditor General. 2022. *Auditor General's Special Report on Procedures Taken to Avoid the Shortage of Pharmaceuticals in Government Hospitals by 13 May 2022.*

About 79% of patients interviewed, however, reported that they experienced some delay in receiving their medicines from the health facility they visited. The waiting time ranged from 30 minutes to 5 hours with a median of 2–3 hours. When patients were asked "Did the health care staff provide clear instructions on how to take your medications?", most patients (93%) responded "No." These findings show that patients were not receiving adequate instructions on the medication they received. This could lead to an unknown proportion of wastage of drugs that can lead to reduced acceptance of the care received.

Figure 8: Patients' Perception on Waiting Time and Instructions Received (%)

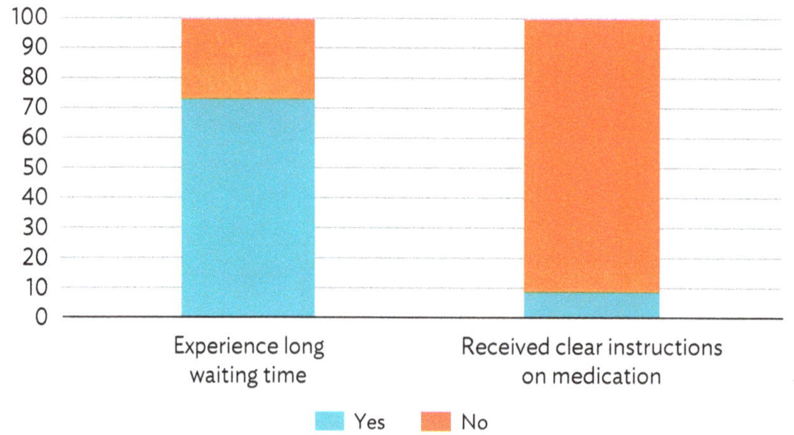

Source: Data collected through the patient satisfaction surveys.

Hospital quality management units are expected to carry out patient satisfaction surveys regularly that assess pharmacy service as one component. All institutions visited were unable to show data on those surveys specifically aiming at pharmacy service.

Box 2 summarizes the issues confronting access in Sri Lanka's pharmaceutical supply chain.

Box 2: Key Identified Gaps in Availability, Accessibility, Affordability, and Acceptability

- Frequent stock out of priority medicines
- 3.5% of total stock (excluding COVID-19 items) was lost due to product expiry
- Around 47% of current health expenditure is out-of-pocket expenditure.
- 34% of out-of-pocket expenditure is spent on pharmaceuticals
- High waiting time for obtaining pharmaceutical services at hospitals
- Inadequate instructions provided to patients during dispensing

COVID-19 = coronavirus disease.
Source: Asian Development Bank assessment team.

5.4 Pharmaceutical Supply Chain Management

The procurement and supply chain management system of MOH can be broken down into eight segments (Figure 9): product selection, qualification, procurement, storage, transportation, end use information, waste disposal, and drug resistance monitoring.

Figure 9: Procurement and Supply Chain Management System of the Ministry of Health

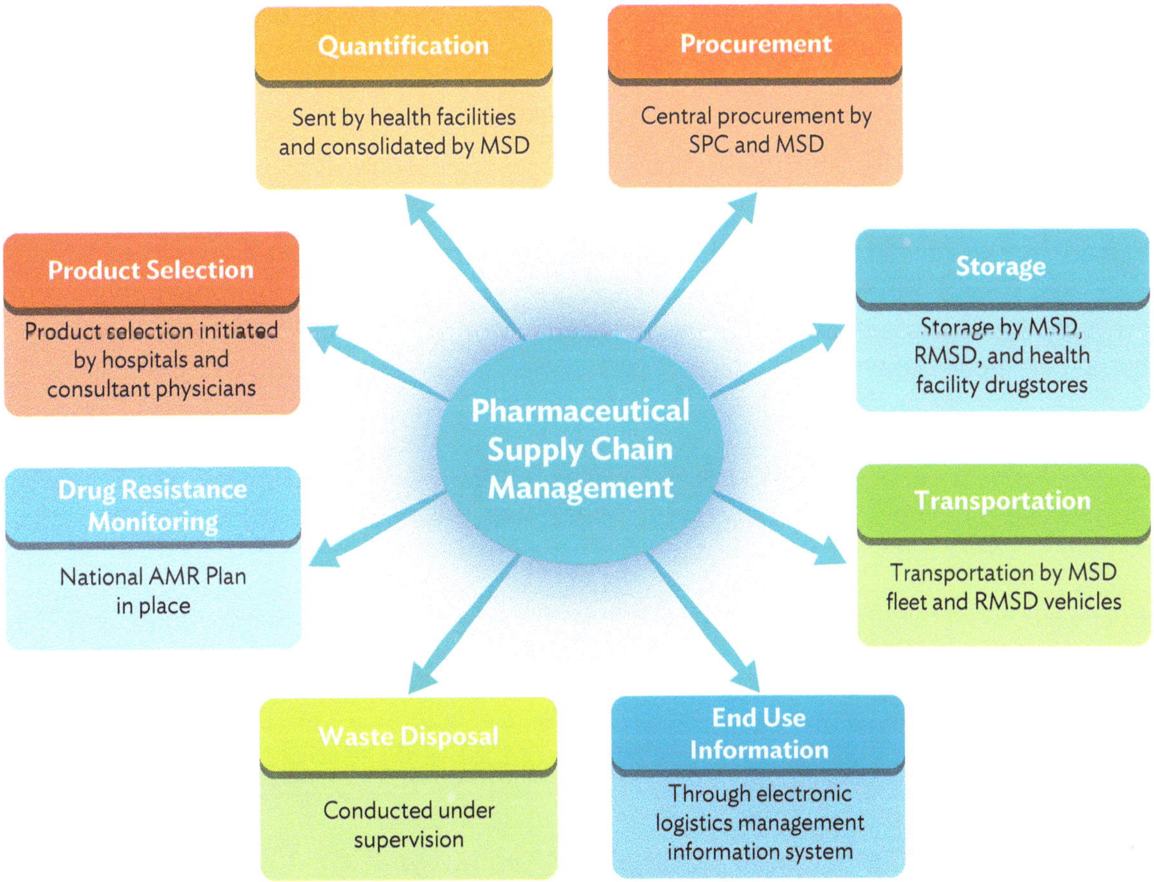

AMR = antimicrobial resistance, MSD = Medical Supplies Division, RMSD = Regional Medical Supplies Division, SPC = State Pharmaceutical Corporation.
Sources: Ministry of Health and Asian Development Bank assessment team.

5.4.1 Product Selection

Product selection refers to selecting products and dosage forms for essential pharmaceutical product lists and deciding which products will be available at each level of the health system. The country procured 1,028 items in 2023, including 850 items from the Priority List dated 4 April 2023.[28] Besides the listed stock items and named patient items in the 2023 priority list, the country needed to procure 178 additional items based on clinical consultants' requests. There is a lack of written policies and criteria for selecting products beyond the EML. Selecting products not included in the EML also indicates missed opportunities for product selection optimization by limiting treatment variations and consolidating total demand for a therapeutic class.

5.4.2 Quantification

Forecasting and supply planning, which is also referred to as quantification, is the process of determining the quantities and timing of supply of products needed to satisfy future demand through scientific and systematic methods. The MSD uses a "pull system" each year to ask for estimates from all hospitals and health facilities and then validates and collates them to develop national annual estimations. Item lists received from health facilities are examined by the specific stock control officer and the assistant director of MSD for list deviations, unrealistic estimations, and approval from institutional national drug and therapeutic committees.

According to the Manual on Management of Drugs,[29] the estimation process begins in August of the current year (year 1) with the preparation of institutional estimates for the next year (year 2). Institutions send their estimates by October of the current year (year 1) to MSD, which consolidates the estimates, forecasts the annual requirements, and places the orders with the SPC by January of next year (year 2). Orders requested for year 2 are scheduled to be supplied during year 3 (Figure 10).

Figure 10: Forecasting, Procurement, and Supply Cycle in Sri Lanka

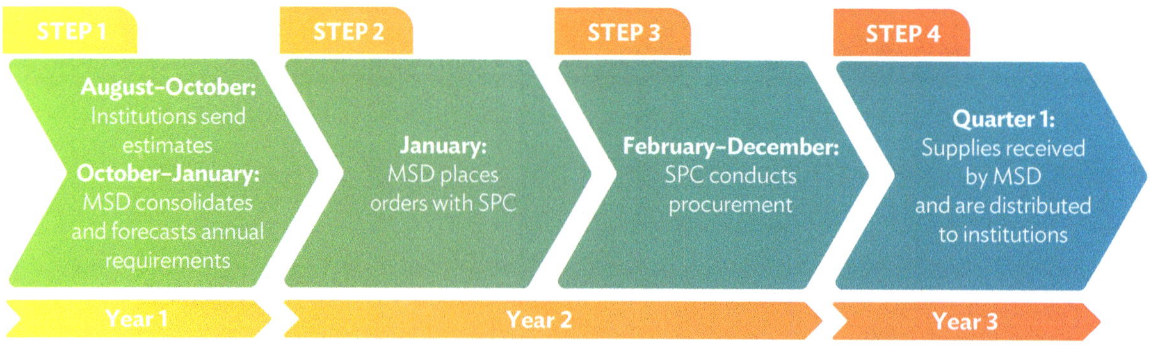

MSD = Medical Supplies Division, SPC = State Pharmaceutical Corporation.
Sources: Ministry of Health and Asian Development Bank assessment team.

[28] Government of Sri Lanka, Ministry of Health. 2023. *Priority List for Pharmaceuticals—Total 850 Items*. Circular No. 01-14/2023. 4 April. Medical Supplies Division.

[29] Government of Sri Lanka, Ministry of Health and Nutrition. 2008. *Manual on Management of Drugs. Second Revision.*

As illustrated in Figure 10, due to long forecasting and procurement lead times, there are mismatches between the forecasting and receiving supply (quantities forecast for year 2 are received in year 3), and between budget and procurement cycle (budget for year 2 is used for receiving items in year 3). The mismatches and long lead time make it extremely challenging to enhance forecast accuracy.

The whole process of consolidating the estimates and placing orders for procurement takes around 6 months and involves pharmacy staff from all health facilities and around 60 stock control officers at MSD. Although consumption data is available at the central level, data analytics is not systematically used. There are no systematic methods or tools used for forecasting and supply planning, and estimation is often based on a mere 10%–15% increase from the previous year's order.

Table 9 provides the percentage of estimate over consumption for a set of 13 vital and 25 most used products from 2019 to 2022.

Table 9: Percentage of Estimate Over Consumption of Tracer Products, 2019–2022

Item	Share (%)			
	2019	2020	2021	2022
Amoxicillin capsule 250 mg	127	180	346	110
Hydrochlorothiazide tablet 25 mg	114	132	164	143
Furosemide (Frusemide) tablet 40 mg	141	136	159	185
Prazosin tablet 1 mg	128	135	206	235
Enalapril tablet 5 mg	147	153	163	166
Losartan Potassium tablet 50 mg	126	133	147	126
Glyceryl Trinitrate tablet 0.5 mg	170	178	181	166
Amlodipine Besylate tablet 5 mg	110	131	165	214
Nifedipine Extended-Release tablet 20 mg	130	159	157	152
Aspirin Enteric coated tablet 75 mg	165	187	170	242
Clopidogrel tablet 75 mg	111	161	153	179
Streptokinase injection 1,500,000 IU	208	513	215	80
Atorvastatin tablet 10 mg	122	140	154	112
Tenecteplase injection 40 mg vial	183	236	227	209
Paracetamol tablet 500 mg	124	185	257	154
Sodium Valproate tablet 200 mg	124	178	163	303
Sodium Chloride for Intravenous Infusion 0.9% w/v, 500 ml bottle	124	181	167	152
Dextrose/Glucose injection 5% w/v 500 ml Bottle	141	254	189	191
Folic Acid tablet 1 mg	157	154	155	144
Disposable intravenous solution giving sets for single use	139	204	179	192
Salbutamol (Albuterol) tablet 2 mg	115	165	260	92
Beclomethasone dry powder capsule 400 mcg	115	149	197	245

continued on next page

Table 9 *continued*

Item	Share (%)			
	2019	2020	2021	2022
Cetirizine tablet 10 mg	147	159	194	142
Chlorphenamine (Chlorpheniramine) tablet 4 mg	116	158	238	120
Adrenaline and/or Epinephrin injection 1 mg/1 ml ampoule	134	168	151	130
Anti-Rabies serum injection 1,000 IU in 5 ml ampoule	245	206	209	242
Gliclazide tablet 40 mg	123	192	177	152
Metformin tablet 500 mg	130	141	155	170
Thyroxine tablet 50 mcg	172	201	142	148
Hydrocortisone Sodium Succinate for injection 100 mg vial	127	224	229	90
Prednisolone tablet 5 mg	120	163	250	111
Domperidone tablet 10 mg	121	173	180	159
Omeprazole capsule or tablet 20 mg	109	141	172	119
Diclofenac tablet 50 mg	141	310	239	178
Atropine Sulphae injection 600 mcg in 1 ml ampoule	152	176	189	166
Suxamethonium (Succinylcholine) Chloride injection 100 mg in 2 ml ampoule	159	180	201	168
Dantroline Sodium injection 20 mg vial	200	252	149	188
Average	**141**	**186**	**191**	**164**

IU = international unit, mcg = microgram, mg = milligram, ml = milliliter.
Source: Data captured in SWASTHA and MSMIS.

It can be noticed that except for a few products where the estimations were lower than actual consumption, in general, estimations were 10%–413% higher than the consumption. The mean variations between the forecast and actual consumption for the set of tracer products presented above indicate an opportunity for efficiency gain through better quantification practices using data analytics and other scientific methods.

5.4.3 Procurement

Procurement refers to the activities associated with acquiring products or services, including procurement planning, sourcing, contract management, receiving, and quality assurance in procurement in line with procurement laws, policies, and regulations.

(i) Procurement by State Pharmaceutical Corporation

The SPC manages sourcing, price negotiation, purchasing, and importation of medical products. SPC purchases products from suppliers and manufacturers with funds received directly from the government Treasury, then settles with the MOH with an additional service charge.

The approach of SPC to procurement is guided by both the National Procurement Agency's 2006 general government standard procurement guidelines, and the 2006 and 2022 Guidelines for Procurement of Pharmaceuticals and Medical Devices.[30] Although the guidelines for procurement of pharmaceuticals asks for prequalification of suppliers and allows flexibility as required by framework agreements with flexible quantities and staggered delivery, SPC solely depends on traditional procurement methods including international competitive bidding, restricted bidding, and direct quotations. It was observed that SPC maintains prequalification only for multisource products for restricted bidding cases and rarely conducts postqualification of suppliers.

(ii) Procurement from State Pharmaceutical Manufacturing Corporation and Local Manufacturers

As mentioned earlier, SPMC enjoys the first right to supply of medicines to MSD. There are 15 other private, registered manufacturers in the country participating in a "buyback" agreement, in which prices for all products are set at a 20% markup over the manufacturing cost. Prices for medicines purchased from Sri Lanka-based manufacturers are set in negotiations among the MOH, Ministry of Trade and Industry, Sri Lanka Pharmaceutical Manufacturers Association, NMRA, and Sri Lanka Standards Institute, MSD and SPC inputs. For products manufactured by SPMC, MSD is authorized to negotiate and purchase directly if SPMC's unit price is lower than the unit price received in the previous tender for the product.

It has been noted that using the first right to supply, SPMC forms joint ventures with local and international manufacturers with local operations to supply medicines to MSD. Although SPMC does not add any value in the joint ventures arrangement, they charge 6% mark-up for the commodities supplied under the joint ventures. Local manufacturers have raised the concern that the first right to supply by SPMC and joint ventures arrangements are distorting a level playing field and fair market competition. Some local experts also said that government should evaluate if the buyback agreement is being implemented as intended.

(iii) Urgent (Emergency) Procurement

"Urgent procurement" is used when there are unforeseen shortages, most often due to quality problems with purchased products. This method allows the government to source "very limited quantities" of an item to cover the gap until the normal supply can be resumed. This approach can also be used on a case-by-case basis for individual patients facing a grave or life-threatening situation. The urgent or emergency procurement is also used when an emergency has been declared by the government due to disasters or disease outbreaks—and for the procurement of single-source products.

30 Government of Sri Lanka, National Procurement Agency. 2006. *Guidelines for Procurement of Pharmaceuticals and Medical Devices*; Government of Sri Lanka. 2022. *Guidelines for Procurement of Pharmaceutical and Medical Devices of a Consumable Nature*.

Although the urgent procurement method should be the exception, frequent use of urgent procurement was observed during the economic crisis period. This reiterates concerns that urgent procurement methods might have been misused in cases of administrative failures other than real emergencies, as regular procurement processes were often delayed or postponed leading to a situation of perpetual emergency to be able to use the urgent procurement methods.

(iv) Local Purchase

The hospitals purchase out-of-stock and urgently needed items at the local level after approval by the hospital administration and MSD. During October 2022–September 2023, the total value of local purchase by hospitals for this 12 months was estimated to be only 1% of the total procurement value of the country, which is much lower than the current share. When asked if the facility did any local purchase of medicines over the past 12 months, only 9 facilities (11%) out of 79 facilities interviewed reported any local purchase. Table 10 presents the list of items procured locally by hospitals and their price comparison with international reference prices.

Table 10: Prices of Items Locally Procured by Hospitals

Item	Unit Price (SLR)	Unit Price ($)	International Reference Price (SLR)	International Reference Price ($)	Share of International Reference Price (%)
Fluorouracil	1,000	3.1	N/A	N/A	N/A
Docetaxel	4,750	14.5	12,960	39.6	37
Irinotrican	300	0.9	1,846	5.6	16
Amiodorone injection	1,150	3.5	320	1.0	360
Sodium bicarbonate injection	550	1.7	1571	4.8	35
Dextrose 25%	69	0.2	N/A	N/A	N/A
Tranexam injection	3,750	11.5	1,696	5.2	221
Dobutamine injection	960	2.9	348	1.1	276
Vasoprasin injection	1,400	4.3	N/A	N/A	N/A
Medizolam injection	882	2.7	N/A	N/A	N/A
Marcain injection	895	2.7	N/A	N/A	N/A
Hydrating wound set	4,317	13.2	N/A	N/A	N/A
Paracitic acid	9,500	29.0	N/A	N/A	N/A
Metachlopramide injection	100	0.3	N/A	N/A	N/A
Iron Sucrose injection	1,633	5.0	1,756	5.4	93
Clarithromycin syrup	896	2.7	858	2.6	104
Ondantrecvin injection	130	0.4	112	0.3	116

N/A = not available, SLR = Sri Lankan rupee.
Note: $1 = SLR327.27 as of 30 October 2023 (source: poundsterlinglive).
Source: Data collected through the facilities assessment interviews.

(v) Procurement Price, Lead Time, and On-Time Delivery

Table 11 presents the total number of procurement orders to be delivered by SPC, SPMC, and MSD from 1 November 2022 to 31 October 2023, actual number of orders delivered, and percentage of international reference price paid for the top 15– 20 items based on volume, unit cost, and procurement value.

Table 11: Procurement Performance and Prices for the Orders to Be Delivered, November 2022–October 2023

	SPC	SPMC	MSD	Total
Number of orders due for delivery	198	289	431	918
Number of orders delivered	130	141	202	473
Share of orders delivered	66%	49%	47%	52%
Average no. of days from order placement to delivery (for the items delivered)	532	251	241	324
Mean share of international reference price paid for top 15–20 *high-volume* procurement	99%	68%	53%	58%
Mean share of international reference price paid for top 15–20 *high-unit-price* procurement	208%	256%	86%	206%
Mean share of international reference price paid for top 15–20 *high-value* procurement	146%	92%	102%	115%

MSD = Medical Supplies Division, SPC = State Pharmaceutical Corporation, SPMC = State Pharmaceutical Manufacturing Corporation.
Source: Analysis of data captured in SWASTHA and Medical Supply Management Information System.

During the economic crisis, MSD and SPC had to extend, postpone, or cancel orders frequently to deal with the foreign currency shortage. Only around 52% of orders placed were delivered (and not necessarily on-time and in-full) according to the delivery schedule.

The price variations compared to international reference prices indicate that the country achieved economies of scale by pooling public sector demand and centrally procuring medicines in bulk. However, the central procurement did not result in cost saving for procuring high-unit-price and low-volume products. Also, for the locally produced high-unit-price and low-volume items, the prices were significantly higher than the international reference price, indicating a lack of economies of scale in producing those items locally for a small market. The nonbulk purchase of named patient drugs by SPC incurred high administrative burdens and did not achieve any economies of scale.

5.4.4 Storage and Transportation

(i) Warehousing and Inventory Control

Warehousing refers to maintenance of storage conditions, including cold chain maintenance from port of entry to end user. It also includes infrastructure facilities and effectiveness of inventory management system. There are nearly 20 bulk warehouses and 5 cold rooms in the MSD central medical stores, providing storage facilities for pharmaceuticals, surgical and medical devices, laboratory chemicals and devices, diagnostic agents and devices, radioactive items, narcotics, and printed forms. Furthermore, there are three bulk warehouses at Angoda, five at Wellawatta, one at Digana, and one at Welisara. The current MSD store capacity is 35,932 cubic meters.[31]

Additionally, MSD has a network of 26 regional warehouses (RMSDs) at the district level. These are managed by the provincial councils of Sri Lanka's nine provinces, which supply the items to health institutions. Each institution has a main drugstore and sub-stores in the indoor and outdoor dispensaries to provide the wards, clinics, and outpatient departments with their requirements.

As can be seen in the result of good storage practice status assessment of pharmaceutical stores in Appendix 2, 93% of facilities had their storage secured under lock and key; 98% of the facilities followed "First Expiry First Out" method to rotate their stock; and 80% conducted regular stock count. However, 91% of the facilities did not specify designated areas for different functions of store management; 98% did not have any smoke detector, fire alarm, and fire safety equipment in place; and 91% did not have any bin cards attached to the stack of products. For a few facilities visited by the assessment team, facilities were asked about the reason for not having a bin card. Facilities mentioned that it was not necessary as they had the information in the SWASTHA electronic system. However, while checking the SWASTHA, the information was not updated. This indicates a weakness in physical inventory management deviating from good storage practices. Most of the stores throughout the supply chain did not maintain basic storage requirements, with 82% of the facilities reporting that they did not follow any policy for minimum and maximum stock of a product to prevent stockout or overstocking.

Using scoring for fully observed, partially observed, and unobserved practices for the 82 stores assessed against 25 criteria provided in Appendix 2, mean percentages of good storage practices were calculated. Table 12 provides a summary of store conditions observed.

Table 12: Good Storage Practices Maintained

Facility Type	No. of Stores Assessed	Mean % of Good Storage Practice Observed
Medical Supplies Division Central	2	70
Regional Medical Supplies Division	1	70
Tertiary care hospitals	5	63
Base hospital A	5	65
Base hospital B	3	69
District hospital A	10	60
District hospital B	15	58
District hospital C	19	51
Primary medical care unit	22	57
TOTAL	**82**	**58**

Source: Analysis of data from store assessment visits.

[31] M. D. A. Krishanth, I. M. S. M. Rajakaruna, and K. E. S. Fernando. 2023. Sensible Factors that Need Strategic Change to Improve the Medical Drug Availability across Healthcare Institutions in Sri Lanka. *International Journal of Current Science Research and Review*. 6 (7). pp. 4721–472.

Overall, 58% of health institutions with good storage practices indicate ample room for improvement. Especially, most of the stores need to install temperature monitors, smoke detectors, fire alarms, location labels, bin cards, and stock cards. Staff need to be trained in good storage and distribution practices.

(ii) Transportation to Dispensing Facilities

Transportation refers to the movement of supplies through a network of transportation and transit points from warehouses to end-users. MSD mostly follows the current administrative network of central, provincial, and district level facilities and transports commodities accordingly. The distribution system is mostly reactive as to receiving and rationing supplies and a "pull system" is used when requests are made by line ministry institutions and RMSDs to the MSD to arrange dispatch of items.

It was observed that vaccines cold chain was well ensured throughout the supply chain with the use of temperature-controlled refrigerators and carrying boxes (supported by UNICEF). However, for other medicines requiring cold chain, there is a risk of breakage of the cold chain during transportation and storage.

Currently, MSD has a fleet of 34 vehicles of which only 50% had air conditioners and around 60% of the air conditioners required repair. More than one-third of the vehicles were more than 30 years old and around one-fourth of the vehicles were not in running condition (under repair). This indicates a serious issue of transporting pharmaceuticals and other medical products in suboptimal and nontemperature-controlled conditions with possible effect on quality, safety, and efficacy of medicines.

The RMSD also reported transport delays due to the limited number of trucks at RMSD. As a result, the receiving facilities often needed to arrange their own transport to pick up supplies from MSD or RMSD.

Due to uncertainty in procuring and receiving commodities, transport schedules were organized on an ad hoc basis requiring more trips than ideally required in an organized fleet management and distribution system. Out of the facilities surveyed, only 15% of orders were delivered on time and in full. Table 13 shows the details of number of items requested by health facilities from MSD or RSMD and number of items received on-time and in-full during the past 12 months.

Table 13: On-Time and In-Full Delivery to Health Facilities

Type of Facility	No. of Responses	No. of Items Ordered	No. of Items Received	OTIF Delivery (%)
Tertiary care	7	3,146	575	18
Base hospital A	6	920	0	0
Base hospital B	3	192	0	0
District hospital A	10	261	28	11
District hospital B	10	712	233	33
District hospital C	12	537	16	3
Primary medical care unit	22	398	89	22
Total	**70**	**6,166**	**941**	**15**

OTIF = on time and in full.
Source: Data collected through the facilities assessment questionnaire and onsite visits.

5.4.5 End Use Information and Digital Information Systems

(i) Logistics Management Information System

Logistics management information system refers to data visibility and use of digital information systems for logistics, and includes timeliness, completeness, accuracy, and use of data collected through the systems. In 2015, MSD officially launched MSMIS (Pronto) that linked MSD with SPC; 26 RMSDs; 57 hospitals; and selected provincial hospitals (base hospitals type A and B, and divisional hospitals). By May 2023, a total of 250 institutions including 204 hospitals were connected to MSMIS (Pronto). However, MSMIS (Pronto) could not provide visible actual consumption data at all health facilities. The drug estimation and verification functions were affected by the unavailability of MSMIS beyond the drug stores of the health care institutions. As a result, data available through MSMIS were not fully used for monitoring, decision making, and forecasting.

The government discontinued the use of MSMIS (Pronto) from July 2023 and introduced a new integrated system for electronic health records and logistics management information system, the SWASTHA.

Patients registered in SWASTHA receive a personal health number (their unique identifying number) and a machine-readable barcode allowing them to seek services from any government health facility. Patients' diagnosis, consultation details, and prescription information are entered in the system during the consultation. SWASTHA connects the electronic health record with the stock on hand from the drug store for the treatment provider. If any prescription medicine is not available for dispensing, SWASTHA shows alternative medicines and their stock. At the drug store and warehouses, SWASTHA captures and continuously updates logistics information such as opening stock, quantity received, quantity issued, any adjustments, and ending balance stock. The system also aggregates information from all reporting facilities and prepares a dashboard for the aggregated status.

SWASTHA opens several potential options for further use of information and data analytics such as the following:

(a) Electronic health records and prescription records can be used for prescription audits and enhancing rational use of medicines.
(b) Electronic prescription and health records from SWASTHA are accessible anywhere and anytime, and any authorized treatment provider can access them to treat patients from any clinic.
(c) SWASTHA can also extrapolate health management information system data from the electronic health records.

As of November 2023, a total of 750 out 1,159 health facilities were using SWASTHA. SWASTHA needs to address the following challenges:

(a) Connect all dispensaries and wards with SWASTHA so that dispensaries and wards can readily access the electronic prescriptions, and items dispensed are automatically deducted from the system to reconcile stock received, stock issued, and stock consumed.

(b) Ensure internet connectivity for all facilities.
(c) Further develop the warehouse management system module to cover all aspects of warehouse management.
(d) Further develop management dashboard and train managers on evidence-based decision making.
(e) Train users on SWASTHA to increase acceptance of the system especially among treatment providers and pharmacists.
(f) Ensure institutional arrangement and sustainability for hosting, maintaining, and continuous upgrading of SWASTHA.

(ii) Other Information System and Data Analytics

Information systems in Sri Lanka's health system, in general, is marked with multiple fragmented and parallel information systems without interoperability and use of data. Overall data analytics and evidence-based decision-making practice could be further strengthened. The country is yet to make data on safety, efficacy, and cost effectiveness of medicines available and used to inform essential medicines selection. The country also needs information systems and enterprise resource planning software for supporting the functions of product registration, procurement, quality assurance, pharmacovigilance, and training.

5.4.5 Waste Disposal

Pharmaceutical waste disposal refers to disposal practices of unused and/or expired medicines. The NMRA Act has a section on pharmaceutical waste disposal. In addition, NMRA developed a guideline in 2021 on Safe Disposal of Expired and Unwanted Pharmaceuticals.[32]

As seen in Table 14, 71% of the facilities interviewed complied with the national guidelines in disposing pharmaceutical wastes.

Table 14: Pharmaceutical Waste Disposal Practice

Type of Facility	Total Responses	Complied	Not complied	Not Applicable	Compliance Rate (%)
Tertiary	7	6	1	0	86
Base hospital A	7	5	1	1	83
Base hospital B	3	2	1	0	67
District hospital A	10	5	5	0	50
District hospital B	12	9	3	0	75
District hospital C	17	8	9	0	47
Primary medical care unit	23	20	2	1	91
Total	**79**	**55**	**22**	**2**	**71**

Source: Data collected through the facilities assessment questionnaire.

32 National Medicines Regulatory Authority. 2021. *Guideline for Safe Disposal of Expired and Unwanted Pharmaceuticals.*

For the facilities that complied with the guidelines, staff actively tracked and documented expired and quality-failed products and pulled them from storage. They either returned the expired or quality-failed items to MSD, RMSD, a higher level facility, or handed over them to a designated company for safe disposal. Another option followed by the facilities was to bury the items under guidance. Facilities that did not comply with the guidelines mentioned that they did not follow any protocol, burned the items in open air, or put them in dustbins with other garbage. There also have been complaints on the delay in organizing a "condemnation committee" and getting their approval for disposing the waste items.

5.4.6 Drug Resistance Monitoring

Drug resistance monitoring refers to the system for monitoring and addressing drug resistance including antimicrobial resistance (AMR). The WHO Expert Committee on Selection and Use of Essential Medicines developed the AWaRe classification of antibiotics in 2017 as a tool to support antibiotic stewardship efforts at local, national, and global levels. According to the AWaRe tool, antibiotics are classified into three groups: access, watch, and reserve, considering the impact of different antibiotics and antibiotic classes on AMR to emphasize the importance of their appropriate use.

Sri Lanka has a National Antimicrobial Resistance Strategic Plan 2017–2022 developed with WHO assistance. However, Sri Lanka's EML did not incorporate WHO's AWaRe classification of antibiotics until April 2024 when the Ministry of Health of Sri Lanka adopted the AWaRe classification through a General Circular issued on 9 April 2024.[33]

All hospitals in Sri Lanka have committees for AMR; however, it was observed that there is no dedicated unit with adequate capacity to implement the national strategy and action plans on AMR at the central level. During the time of finalization of this report, the country was in the process of launching the National Strategic Plan for Combating Antimicrobial Resistance, and National Action Plan with Monitoring and Evaluation Parameters for the period 2023–2028.

Box 3 summarizes the challenges in Sri Lanka's pharmaceutical supply chain management.

[33] Government of Sri Lanka, Ministry of Health. 2024. *Implementation of "AWaRe Classification" of Antimicrobials in Healthcare Institutions in Sri Lanka*. General Circular No. 01-13/2024. 9 April.

Box 3: Key Identified Gaps in Pharmaceutical Supply Chain Management in Sri Lanka

- Medicines optimization for minimizing treatment variations and demand consolidation in the product selection process can be further improved
- Inadequate use of available data and scientific methods for forecasting and supply planning
- Long procurement lead time and non-utilization of strategic procurement and framework agreements
- Gaps in the compliance on good storage practices
- Suboptimal transportation condition that may affect the quality, safety, and efficacy of medicines
- Evidence-based decision-making practice can be further supported by using end user information and consumption data
- Low laboratory capacity to carry out drug resistance monitoring activities

Source: The Asian Development Bank assessment team.

5.5 Enabler Factors

5.5.1 Governance—Policy and Regulatory Framework

Governance is defined as the instruments and mechanisms used by national governments and other organizations to set standards and ensure accountability to achieve a defined outcome.

(i) Structure

The current configuration of the governance, policies, and regulatory framework consists of NMRA as the regulatory unit, MSD as the logistics unit, SPC as the procurement unit, health facilities as service delivery units, and a few committees including the National Drug Therapeutic Committee, formulary revision committee, and medical supply review committee. It is, however, not clear which unit is particularly responsible for the overall governance of the pharmaceutical supply chain and monitoring its performance. While the roles of procurement and logistics management are segregated between SPC and MSD, the roles of technical standards setting, policy making, and oversight are not clearly separated with a mechanism for ensuring accountability. This creates a vulnerability for the pharmaceutical supply chain, which was reported to be affected by external interferences and irregularities during the economic crisis period. There is a need for clearly segregating the roles of leadership and oversight, technical standard setting, policy making, regulating, market shaping, procurement, and logistics management with adequate coordination and accountability to make the pharmaceutical supply chain structures work more effectively.

(ii) Monitoring and Evaluation

Currently, there are no formal systems, processes, and tools in place to track end-to-end supply chain performance. There is no policy or strategy that sets standards for collection and management of pharmaceutical supply chain information for monitoring and evaluation.

(iii) Procurement Policy

Table 15 summarizes the current procurement policies and practices in Sri Lanka against key assessment criteria.

Table 15: Current Procurement Policies and Practices

	Criteria	Question	Max Score	Obtained Score	Remarks
1	Alignment with international best practices	How well do the guidelines align with internationally recognized best practices for pharmaceutical procurement?	3	2	Partially follows guidelines of the World Health Organization for good procurement practices
2	Responsiveness to local context	To what extent do the guidelines consider the unique challenges and characteristics of the local health care system?	3	3	Protects local manufacturing through buy back arrangement
3	Clarity of procedures	How clear and well-defined are the procurement procedures outlined in the guidelines?	3	2	The country does not follow manufacturer level prequalification procedures for all health product procurement
4	Inclusion of sustainable procurement principles	Do the guidelines incorporate principles of sustainability, including environmental, social, and economic considerations?	3	1	Very little or no mention of environmental considerations and sustainable procurement practices
5	Consideration of public health needs	How effectively do the guidelines address the procurement of essential medicines and medical products that are critical to public health?	3	2	Although the guidelines allow framework agreements to better respond to variable public health needs, framework agreements are not practiced yet
6	Adaptability to changing circumstances	How flexible are the guidelines in adapting to changing health care demands, technological advancements, and unforeseen disruptions?	3	2	Emergency procurement allows adapting to changing circumstances but overuse of emergency procurement compromises the purpose of procurement guidelines
		TOTAL	**18**	**12**	**67%**

Scoring scale: 0 = not addressed, 1 = partially addressed, 2 = adequately addressed, 3 = fully addressed.
Source: Assessment team's evaluation.

The current procurement policies and guidelines need to be updated to incorporate green and sustainable procurement and move from a traditional market-dependent approach of procurement to a more strategic and market-shaping approach.

(iv) Drug Regulation and Registration

As presented in Table 16, the average number of days for decision making on an application for medicine registration took 465 days in the latest 10 cases prior to 11 November 2023.

Table 16: Number of Days Taken for Decision-Making on Registration

	Product Name	Application Type	Application Submission Date	Date of Evaluation	Days Taken for Evaluation
1	Sulfasalazine Delayed Release tablet USP 1000 mg	New (foreign, site change)	28 Jan 2022	11 Nov 2023	652
2	Mycophenolic Acid Delayed Release tablet USP 180 mg	New (foreign)	20 Jun 2022	3 Oct 2023	470
3	Terbutaline Sulfate Syrup 1.5 mg/5 ml	New (foreign, priority)	29 Apr 2022	21 Sep 2023	510
4	Inactivated Influenza (Vaccine Surface Antigen) IP (Quadrivalent)	New (strain variation)	31 Mar 2023	15 Sep 2023	168
5	Linagliptin tablet 5 mg	New (foreign)	14 Mar2022	6 Sep 2023	541
6	Empagliflozin tablet 10 mg	New (foreign, site change)	9 May 2022	24 Aug 2023	472
7	Meloxicam tablet USP 15 mg	New (foreign, site change)	4 Mar 2022	17 Jun 2023	470
8	Alprazolam tablet USP 0.25 mg	New (foreign, site change)	25 Feb 2022	6 Jun 2023	466
9	Lamotrigine tablet USP 50 mg	New (foreign, site change)	22 Dec 2021	23 May 2023	517
10	Cefotaxime for injection USP 1 gram	New (foreign)	22 Mar 2022	10 Apr 2023	384
					Average: 465 days

IU = international unit, mcg = microgram, mg = milligram, ml = milliliter, USP = United States Pharmacopeia.
Source: National Medicines Regulatory Authority.

However, NMRA has been working on improving its decision-making process. More recent data shared by NMRA, as presented in Table 17, shows that the average decision-making time for NMRA for the last 10 cases prior to 21 May 2024 was reduced to 342 days.

Table 17: Number of Days Taken for Decision-Making on Registration, 2024

	Product Name	Application Submission Date	Date of Evaluation	Number of Calendar Days
1	Levodopa 200 mg and Benserazide 50 mg tablets	1 Apr 2024	21 May 2024	50
2	Cyclophosphamide injection IP 500 mg	21 Sep 2020	30 Jan 2024	1,226
3	Chlorpheniramine Maleate oral solution USP 2 mg/5 ml	25 Sep 2023	1 Mar 2024	158
4	Lidocaine injection BP 2% w/v	13 Jun 2023	22 Jan 2024	223
5	Losartan Potassium tablets USP 25 mg	10 Aug 2023	8 May 2024	272
6	Amoxicillin capsule BP 250 mg	8 Apr 2022	10 May 2024	763
7	Eptacog Alfa Powder for solution for injection 1.2 mg	22 Nov 2023	21 May 2024	181
8	Sitagliptin tablets USP 50 mg	16 Jan 2023	20 Feb 2024	400
9	Co-Amoxiclav for injection BP 1.2 g	1 Sep 2023	10 Jan 2024	131
10	Pentoxifylline Extended-Release tablets USP 400 mg	3 May 2024	21 May 2024	18
				Average: 342 days

G=gram, IU = international unit, mcg = microgram, mg = milligram, ml = milliliter, USP = United States Pharmacopeia, w/v = weight per volume.
Source: National Medicines Regulatory Authority.

It was found that the common technical dossier (CTD) used by NMRA was not harmonized with the format of the International Council on Harmonization for registration of pharmaceuticals as well as with the Association of Southeast Asian Nations CTD format. For registering generic medicines, Sri Lanka requests bioequivalence studies for antimicrobials, antiepileptic drugs, and narrow therapeutic index drugs and does not accept bio-waiver at present. Although NMRA is recognizing accelerated product registration pathway using WHO prequalification dossiers, Sri Lanka's drug regulatory system is not fully streamlined with that of higher-income countries and does not yet practice reliance on stringent decisions made by regulatory authorities.[34]

5.5.2 Human Resources—People and Practice

Human resources for the pharmaceutical supply chain refer to the knowledge, capability, and availability of a workforce to implement and execute pharmaceutical supply chain functions within the pharmaceutical supply chain management system.

For line MOH-managed hospitals and MSD, a total of 1,234 pharmacist positions out of 1,406 approved positions were filled with licensed pharmacists, leaving 12% vacancies (Table 18).

Table 18: Pharmacist Positions for Institutions Owned by the Ministry of Health

Facility	Total Positions	Filled Positions	Vacancies
Medical Supplies Division	51	47	4
National Hospital of Sri Lanka	100	97	3
National Hospital of Kandy	95	78	17
Teaching Hospital Karapitiya	60	57	3
Teaching Hospital Kerunegala	56	45	11
Teaching Hospital Colombo South Kalubowla	49	47	2
Teaching Hospital Anuradhapura	48	46	2
Teaching Hospital Kalutara	46	32	14
District General Hospital Ampara	46	27	19
Teaching Hospital Colombo North Ragama	45	41	4
Apeksha Hospital Maharagama	45	39	6
Others	765	678	87
Total	**1,406 (100%)**	**1,234 (88%)**	**172 (12%)**

Source: Ministry of Health.

[34] D. Thambavita, P. Galappatthy, and R. L. Jayakody. 2018. Regulatory Requirements for the Registration of Generic Medicines and Format of Drug Dossiers: Procedures in Sri Lanka in Comparison with Selected Regulatory Authorities. *Journal of Pharmaceutical Policy and Practice*. 11 (1).

However, as shown in Table 19, at the subnational level (excluding tertiary care facilities) that are managed by provincial councils, there were higher vacancy rates (22%) for pharmacists and dispensing staff in the health facilities assessed.

Table 19: Pharmaceutical Supply Management Positions at Subnational Level

Type of Facility	No. of Responses	Total Positions	Filled Positions	Vacancies
Base hospital A	7	85	67	18
Base hospital B	3	18	16	2
District hospital A	10	48	31	17
District hospital B	10	36	30	6
District hospital C	17	39	28	11
Primary medical care unit	28	28	25	3
Total	**75**	**254 (100%)**	**197 (78%)**	**57 (22%)**

Source: Data collected through the facilities assessment questionnaire.

While the tertiary care facilities have approved positions for chief pharmacist, pharmacy in charge, pharmacist, and dispenser; at the secondary care facilities pharmaceutical supply management positions are filled in by pharmacists, dispensers, and support staff. At primary medical care units, there is no position for a licensed pharmacist. Drug store management and dispensing is handled by a dispenser and/or a medical officer at the primary medical care units. Many of the pharmaceutical supply chain positions are filled in by staff with no professional training on pharmaceutical supply chain at all.

Bachelor of pharmacy programs were only introduced in Sri Lanka in 2006 in two Sri Lankan universities, University of Peradeniya and University of Sri Jayewardenepura. With the addition of the bachelor of pharmacy program offered by the University of Colombo and University of Jaffna, there are currently four universities in Sri Lanka that offer a degree program in pharmacy.[35] In addition, the Kothelawela Defence University managed by the Ministry of Defence offers a bachelor of pharmacy degree for civilian students. However, the pharmacy bachelor's degree curriculum in Sri Lanka does not include any course on pharmaceutical supply chain and there is no preservice training or academic course currently available in Sri Lanka on pharmaceutical supply chain management. That means many of the members of the pharmaceutical supply chain workforce in Sri Lanka lack a basic degree in pharmacy and none of the members of the pharmaceutical supply chain workforce has ever received any training related to pharmaceutical supply chain management.

Box 4 contains the personnel issues and policy and regulatory framework issues Sri Lanka faces in its pharmaceutical supply chain.

[35] Government of Sri Lanka, Ministry of Education. 2024. Database of Universities and Institutes (accessed 18 July 2024).

Box 4: Key Identified Gaps in Governance and Human Resources

- The governance structure of pharmaceutical supply chain management requires segregation of leadership, technical standard setting, policy making, regulatory, market shaping, procurement, and logistics management roles with adequate coordination and accountability to reduce the vulnerabilities from external influence and irregularities
- There are no dedicated units for leadership, clinical standards, Essential Medicine List, antimicrobial resistance, and rational use of medicines
- Gaps in oversight, accountability, and monitoring and evaluation framework for the pharmaceutical supply chain
- Strategic procurement practices not introduced comprehensively
- Product registration process does not include reliance pathways to recognize product registration by stringent regulatory authority
- No academic courses or preservice and in-service training available on pharmaceutical supply chain management

Source: Asian Development Bank assessment team.

5.6 Market Ecosystem

The value of Sri Lanka's pharmaceutical market was estimated to be approximately SLR163 billion, or around $449 million in 2022.[36] With 83.6% dependency on imported products for pharmaceuticals, and 100% dependency on imported active pharmaceutical ingredients for local manufacture of medical products, Sri Lanka's pharmaceutical supply chain is highly volatile to foreign currency reserve, currency exchange, and regional and global pharmaceutical supply chain fluctuations.

The SPMC currently manufactures 66 medical products, including 42 items of medicines, and supplies 85% of its products to the state. Local manufacturers, SPMC, and joint ventures currently manufacture 250 items out of the total 850 items in the Priority List (Table 20).

Table 20: Local Manufacturing of Essential Medicines

Manufacturer	No. of Items Manufactured	No. of Items in Priority List	Priority List Items Manufactured Locally (%)
State Pharmaceutical Manufacturing Corporation	42	850	5
Local manufacturers	98	850	12
Joint venture	110	850	13
Total	**250**	**850**	**30**

Source: Data provided by private sector.

36 Sri Lanka Association of Clinical Pharmacology and Therapeutics. Evidence Synthesis on Essential Medicines Policy Reform Options for Sri Lanka. World Health Organization (Project No. 2022/1279296-0). $1 = SLR363.11 as of 31 December 2022 (source: Central Bank of Sri Lanka).

As mentioned earlier, local manufacturers enjoy a negotiated price and buy-back guarantee and do not compete with international suppliers. However, due to the small local market, local manufacturers cannot achieve economies of scale for low-volume, high-unit-price products. The unit prices of such low-volume and high-unit-price locally manufactured products were much higher than the international reference prices. Although the government is envisioning export of medicines to the international market, local manufacturers believe that they still need to go a long way in terms of assuring quality standards and gaining international confidence on the quality assurance provided by NMRA to achieve that vision.

Apart from limited price-regulating practices by NMRA, the country does not employ any other pricing or market-shaping strategies. Despite the government's intentions to take part in international pooled procurement mechanisms to enhance the availability and affordability of medical products, there are no readily available and suitable regional or international pooled procurement mechanisms that could adequately address the need for Sri Lanka's pharmaceutical procurement.

According to the NMRA, many essential pharmaceutical products in Sri Lanka did not have enough registered suppliers and even registered suppliers sometimes did not take part in procurement bidding due to nonavailability of ready stock and delayed payment. The lack of a sufficient number of registered products and suppliers taking part in procurement bidding makes it more challenging to ensure availability and competitive price of the pharmaceutical products. There is a need for further research to understand the challenges and barriers for both domestic and international manufacturers and suppliers for market access and how to address those barriers for greater availability and market shaping.

5.7 Summary: Performance Against Selected Key Indicators

Table 21 summarizes the performance of Sri Lanka's pharmaceutical industry while Box 5 summarizes the constraints in the marketing of locally manufactured pharmaceutical products in Sri Lanka.

Table 21: Performance Against Selected Key Indicators

Area	Indicator	Finding
Appropriate use of medicines	Percentage availability of National Treatment Guidelines that have been reviewed or updated within the past 3 years	Ad hoc basis
Appropriate use of medicines	Percentage of medicines prescribed according to National Treatment Guidelines	Not monitored
Quality	Percentage of samples received by the NMQAL tested that failed quality control testing	Result removed due to the non-availability of representative denominators
Safety: Pharmacovigilance	Percentage of recorded adverse event reports that were assessed for causality	89.5% (300/335)
Efficacy	Presence of an EML	Yes
Availability	Proportion of health facilities that have a core set of relevant essential medicines (according to the National Formulary) available and affordable on a sustainable basis	11.5%

continued on next page

Table 21 *continued*

Area	Indicator	Finding
Availability	Percentage of product losses by value due to expired medicines or damage or theft per value received	3.7% (4.06/110)
Service delivery and accessibility	Average distance of households from a dispensing facility or pharmacy	5 kilometers
Finance and affordability	Out-of-pocket expenditure on pharmaceuticals out of total out-of-pocket expenditure for health	34%
Acceptability	Percentage of patients surveyed who are satisfied with pharmaceutical services from their last visit to a public health facility	81% (88/108)
Product selection	Percentage of medicines selected from EML over the total number of medicines procured	82.6% (850/1,028) (priority list)
Forecasting and supply planning	Mean percentage of variation between the forecast and actual consumption for a set of tracer products	64%
Procurement	Percentage of median international price paid for a set of tracer medicines that was part of the last procurement	96%
Procurement	Percentage of supplier with on-time and in-full delivery (disaggregated by three types of procurement: regular procurement, local procurement, and emergency procurement)	51.5% (500/969)
Warehouse and distribution	Percentage of key storage conditions satisfied	58%
Warehouse and distribution	Percentage of orders received on-time and in-full	15% (941/6,166)
Warehouse and distribution	Percentage of temperature-controlled vehicles in the total distribution fleet	50% (17/34)
End use: logistics management information system	Percentage of health facilities that submit complete logistics management information system reports on time to their reporting unit	64.7% (750/1,159)
Information system	Data on safety, efficacy, and cost effectiveness of medicines available and used to inform essential medicines selection	No
End use: drug resistance monitoring	Percentage of key action items implemented from the National Action Plan on Antimicrobial Resistance	Unknown
End use: waste disposal	Percentage of pharmaceutical wastes disposed according to the appropriate guidelines	71%
Governance, policies, and regulatory framework	• Existence of a policy or strategy that sets standards for collection and management of pharmaceutical supply chain information for monitoring and evaluation • Index to assess the relevance and appropriateness of the current pharmaceutical procurement guidelines in meeting the specific needs and challenges of the health care system • Average number of days for decision making on a medicine application for registration	• No • 67% (12/18) • 342
Human resources	Proportion of pharmaceutical supply chain positions that are filled in with licensed pharmacists, pharmacy technicians, or pharmacy assistants	MOH: 88% (1,234/1,406) Subnational: 78% (197/254)
Market ecosystem	Percentage of products on the EML that are currently manufactured or co-manufactured within the country	30% (250/850)

EML = Essential Medicine List, MOH = Ministry of Health, NMQAL = National Medicine Quality Assurance Laboratory.
Source: Asian Development Bank assessment team.

Box 5: Key Identified Gaps in Market Ecosystem

- Small local market for local manufacturers to achieve economies of scale for low-volume products
- Low supplier interest to register products and to take part in bidding
- Limited use of market-shaping strategies
- Suitable regional and international pooled procurement mechanisms are not available
- Export of domestically manufactured products is limited

Source: Asian Development Bank assessment team.

Chapter 6

DISCUSSION

Thanks to the presence of a government health facility within 5 kilometers of the population and provisions for free medicines, Sri Lanka has achieved high accessibility and affordability of medical products contributing to high patient satisfaction. However, the country can further improve its pharmaceutical supply chain management system to ensure quality and availability of medicines and other medical products in a more cost-effective manner.

As presented in Table 22, Sri Lanka needs to weigh the advantages and disadvantages in choosing its options for upgrading its pharmaceutical supply chain.

Table 22: Different Models of Pharmaceutical Supply Chain

Type of Supply Chain	Characteristics	Strengths	Weaknesses
Medical Supplies Division-led (current status)	• Centrally managed quantification, procurement, and distribution through a central medical store and subsequent supply chain tiers (e.g., regional medical store, hospital drug store)	• Achieves economies of scale in procurement; committed to supply to all over the country	• Long lead time, inefficient distribution network, high stockholding cost
Vertical program-led (e.g., vaccine supply chain led by Epidemiology Unit)	• Supply chain is fragmented or segmented with multiple top-down pharmaceutical supply chains led by vertical programs (e.g., immunization supply chain, HIV supply chain, tuberculosis supply chain, malaria supply chain, noncommunicable diseases supply chain, etc.)	• Close monitoring of supply chain; provides increased efficiency and speed to some extent	• Additional burden on lower-level facilities in managing multiple supply chains; increased supply chain costs
Central framework with decentralized procurement (e.g., E-Katalog of Indonesia)	• Central negotiation and framework agreements with decentralized procurement and order fulfilment directly by suppliers	• Reduced stockholding and distribution costs; Reduced lead time due to framework agreements and direct delivery	• Lack of priority by suppliers to supply low volumes and to geographically remote areas

continued on next page

Table 22 *continued*

Type of Supply Chain	Characteristics	Strengths	Weaknesses
Local purchase through contracted pharmacies	• Central prequalification and framework agreements with local pharmacies • Reimbursement by central body or direct procurement by the health facilities from the prequalified pharmacies at agreed price	• Reduced stockholding and distribution costs • Reduced lead time • Just-in-time access to required medicines	• Pharmacies may not be available in geographically remote areas • Possibility of stockout at the listed pharmacy
Outsourcing to 3PL and 4PL	• Procurement and supply chain functions are partially or fully outsourced to 3PL or 4PL providers that extend professional procurement service to pool demands, conduct procurement, and supply to the government or health facilities	• Increased efficiency and accountability	• Lack of 3PL and 4PL providers and capacity

3PL = third party logistics, 4PL = fourth party logistics.
Source: Asian Development Bank assessment team.

Some of these pharmaceutical supply chain model options are further elaborated in section 6.3. Apart from choosing a pharmaceutical supply chain model, the country could address the following issues identified through this assessment: (i) governance and rational product selection, (ii) forecasting and strategic procurement, (iii) warehousing and distribution, and (iv) use of data for decision-making.

6.1 Governance and Rational Product Selection

Conclusion 1: Increase efficiency and cost-effectiveness of pharmaceutical supply chain

Segregation of leadership and oversight, technical standard setting, policy making, regulatory, market shaping, procurement, and logistics management roles with adequate coordination and accountability within the pharmaceutical supply chain is inadequate. Weak monitoring of rational use of medicines; lack of optimized product selection; ad hoc maintenance of national treatment guidelines; and lack of adequate institutional mechanisms for the EML are creating pressure in procuring an increased number of medicine variations, splitting the demand in a relatively small medicines market, and affecting economies of scale.

There is a need for further clarity and segregation of leadership and oversight, technical standards setting, policy making, regulatory, market shaping, procurement, and logistics management roles with adequate coordination and accountability to reduce the vulnerability of being affected by external influence and corruption.

The opportunities for streamlined product selection and optimization need to be explored further as national treatment guidelines have not been updated for a long time and simple protocols are not adequately adopted to minimize product variations under a therapeutic class. There is no dedicated unit or institution to set up the national treatment standards and their adherence to prevent irrational prescription or overprescribing. There is no practice of prescription audits and clinical review of named patient medicines; neither is there routine surveillance in place for monitoring drug resistance and therapeutical efficacy.

A dedicated unit for health technology assessment, health economics, or pharmacoeconomics to support assessment and selection of medicines for EML is yet to be formed. The EML is practically expanded with a high level of inclusion of additional products based on specialist physicians' recommendations.

The specialist and technical functions of maintaining national treatment guidelines, EML, health technology assessment, national drug and therapeutic committee, and formulary review committee need to be fully segregated and can be assigned to a specialist unit within MOH; or as recommended by the public expenditure review committee, given to a specialist institute. Alternatively, such functions can be performed by strengthening relevant existing committees with clearly defined roles and responsibilities, appropriate membership, training, and tools.

As evidenced in Case Highlights 1, streamlining governance structure and treatment protocols, choosing fewer products, and ensuring rational use of medicines increase efficiency and cost-effectiveness of the pharmaceutical supply chain.

Case Highlights 1: Delhi, India—Rational Use of Medicines

In Delhi, India, a 1997 comprehensive drug policy included the development of an Essential Drugs List, a central pooled procurement system, and programmatic activities to promote rational drug use. This policy demonstrated 30% savings on the cost of drugs to the Delhi government, and increased the availability of key drugs from 40%–70% before the policy's implementation to >90% after its implementation.

Source: Asian Development Bank assessment team.

6.2 Forecasting and Strategic Procurement

Conclusion 2: Increasing suppliers' interest in accessing markets reduces price and ensures availability of products

Lengthy and suboptimal process of forecasting, long procurement lead time, and absence of effective procurement strategies and supply planning are contributing to inefficient procurement, frequent emergency situations, shortage of supply, and higher prices.

The long time spent in collecting, validating, and collating the estimates from health facilities, which information is readily available at the central level through the electronic system, could be easily avoided. Using data from the electronic system and organizing a centrally managed forecasting and supply planning exercise could contribute to increased efficiency in terms of time, effort, and cost.

The long procurement lead time caused by traditional and single item bidding and associated administrative processes is creating a mismatch between forecast period and actual time for receiving supplies, and often leads to shortage of supply and a situation of emergency.

As presented in Case Highlights 2 for Pharmac New Zealand, evidence shows that proactive engagement with manufacturers and suppliers, employing strategic procurement, and using market shaping strategies increases suppliers' interest in accessing markets, reduces prices, and ensures availability of products.

Case Highlights 2: Pharmac New Zealand—Streamlined Product Selection and Pricing Strategies

Pharmac, New Zealand's government agency responsible for procuring pharmaceuticals for the public health system, adopted a centralized product selection process where a committee of experts evaluates and selects medicines based on their therapeutic value and cost-effectiveness. This process allows for rigorous assessment of pharmaceuticals before they are included in the National Formulary. Pharmac also negotiates prices directly with suppliers to achieve cost savings and employs several pricing strategies to reduce the cost of medicines.

Some of Pharmac's key pricing strategies include the following:

- ***Reference pricing.*** Pharmac uses reference pricing as a strategy to set the price of a medicine based on the price of equivalent or similar medicines in other countries with similar health care systems.
- ***Negotiation and tendering.*** Pharmac negotiates directly with pharmaceutical companies to secure competitive prices for medicines. The agency often invites pharmaceutical companies to submit tenders, allowing them to compete on price for supplying specific medicines.

continued on next page

Case Highlights 2 *continued*

- ***Volume agreements.*** Pharmac negotiates volume agreements with pharmaceutical companies, which involve committing to purchase a certain quantity of a medicine over a specified period. In exchange, pharmaceutical companies offer lower prices due to the guaranteed sales volume.

- ***Risk-sharing agreements.*** In some cases, Pharmac establishes risk-sharing agreements with pharmaceutical companies. These agreements tie the reimbursement of a medicine to its performance, efficacy, and outcomes in real-world patient populations. If the medicine does not deliver the expected results, the price paid by Pharmac may be adjusted accordingly.

- ***Parallel imports.*** Pharmac allows parallel imports, which means that wholesalers can import the same medicine from other countries where it is sold at a lower price.

- ***Reference pricing groups.*** Pharmac groups together medicines that are considered therapeutically equivalent or interchangeable. It then sets a single subsidy level for all medicines within the reference pricing group, which helps reduce costs by promoting the use of the most cost-effective medicine within each group.

- ***Delisting and subsidy changes.*** Pharmac regularly reviews the medicines listed on its Pharmaceutical Schedule. If a medicine's cost-effectiveness or clinical benefit is called into question, Pharmac may delist it or change its subsidy status, which can lead to cost savings.

- ***Generic substitution.*** Pharmac promotes the use of generic medicines by subsidizing them at a cost lower than their brand-name equivalents. This encourages health care professionals to prescribe and patients to use these more cost-effective alternatives.

Results

- Through direct negotiations with suppliers, Pharmac has consistently achieved lower prices for pharmaceuticals compared to international benchmarks.

- By focusing on cost-effectiveness and therapeutic value, Pharmac ensures that medicines with the most benefit to patients are included in the formulary, promoting equitable access for all New Zealanders.

- The centralized selection process streamlines procurement by eliminating redundancy and duplication.

Source: Asian Development Bank assessment team.

6.3 Warehousing and Distribution

Conclusion 3: Reduce the risk of quality loss and stockholding costs

The current storage and distribution network could be further optimized for supply chain efficiency by direct delivery to health facilities or by reducing the number of tiers in the supply chain to reduce the risk of quality loss and stock holding costs.

Suboptimal storage and transportation practices potentially affect the quality, safety, and efficacy of medical products. Sri Lanka's current distribution network is not optimized for supply chain efficiency with its limited use of direct delivery and staggered delivery to health facilities. The opportunity for engaging third party logistics to increase efficiency and cut costs in government-owned logistics operations is underexplored. The long procedural delay for disposing pharmaceutical and other items contributes to situations where disposable items occupy spaces in drugstores.

Following on from Table 20, following are some of the options from global practices that can be explored for cost-benefit and cost-effectiveness analysis for a redesigned warehousing and distribution network.

(i) **Option 1: Segmented supply chain**

Supply chain segmentation is the process of dividing the supply chain into distinct, manageable segments. It involves identifying, analyzing, and segmenting the supply chain into distinct markets, channels, and customer groups. The purpose of segmentation is to enable organizations to align the supply chain with customer needs, identify and reduce sources of waste, and increase efficiency and cost savings.[37] One option is to segment the pharmaceutical supply chain management organizations based on type of product, such as vaccines, communicable diseases, and noncommunicable diseases. Their inventory and stock control systems including minimum and maximum stock, replenishment period, and emergency order point should be clearly established and aligned with the procurement and supply cycles to avoid ad hoc distributions. Case Highlights 3 illustrates a noteworthy application.

Case Highlights 3: National Immunization Program in Sri Lanka

Sri Lanka's Expanded Programme on Immunization (EPI) is cited regionally and globally as a successful model due to its strong political and financial commitment, high immunization coverage of essential vaccines, and low incidence of vaccine-preventable diseases. Against all the challenges from the coronavirus disease pandemic, economic crisis, and supply chain issues, EPI maintained high coverage (98%–100%) of all scheduled vaccines.

continued on next page

[37] GEP. 2023. Supply Chain Segmentation.

Case Highlights 3 *continued*

Although the procurement and supply chains of medical products are mostly centralized, Sri Lanka's EPI has established a segmented supply chain by actively contributing and controlling selection of products, quantification of needs, quality assurance during procurement (selected supplier and products need signing off by chief epidemiologist before awarding the purchase order to ensure quality), and delivery schedules. Following are some other good practices identified as factors contributing to the success of EPI in Sri Lanka.[a]

At the national level, the immunization program is managed by the National Epidemiological Service and Family Health Bureau. At the district and grassroots levels, immunization services are fully integrated into public primary preventive health care, which provides preventive care services via a network of Medical Officer of Health areas dividing the entire country to 356 areas. The monitoring and evaluation of grassroots-level immunization activities occur through routine surveillance and periodic reviews. Immunization is integrated into maternal and child health activities and delivery is fully integrated into the overall primary preventive health care package of services. Provision of health education to improve knowledge on disease transmission is handled through the Health Promotion Bureau. The medical specialists (Epidemiologists) working at the national level are engaged in full-time management of immunization related work. In addition to the doctors, all other field public health workers are also trained by the Ministry of Health (MOH) at the National Institute of Health Sciences in Kalutara. This sets the foundation for strong public health functions, including immunization, in Sri Lanka.

To ensure regular funding for immunization, the MOH has historically had a dedicated budget line for vaccine procurement, which means that the core EPI vaccine costs are funded wholly from domestic resources. The training for health professionals incorporates education on counselling patients and families on vaccine hesitancy. The accountability system ensures that there is always somebody who is responsible for those who refuse vaccination.

The national facility network covers the whole island, and there are specially trained staff categories, such as public health inspectors and midwives, available at each level in the health system to support close monitoring, evaluation, and feedback. Periodic surveys are carried out by the public health midwives postvaccination, and they maintain an immunization registry, which includes the next vaccination dates and the children who have missed a dose. This registry is compiled and sent to the MOH to be analyzed, after which the data is sent to the Epidemiology Unit for MOH review.

Role delineation at the health facility level is strong, which helps ensure that each professional fully understands their role and associated responsibilities. Data is discussed in monthly staff meetings, and due to the data analysis being a part of the postgraduate medicine training, most health professionals understand how to use data to improve their health service delivery.

An annual Epidemiology Unit Vaccine-Preventable Disease review is conducted in each district by the central Epidemiology Unit, the regional epidemiologists, and a provincial consultant community physician. In the district, data is collected and presented at all levels.

The community, including local authorities and teachers, are invited to attend monthly meetings conducted at the MOH offices to discuss questions or raise any issue of concern over health service delivery within the area.

---

[a] A. Gamage et al. 2021. *Country Case Study: Lessons Learned from Sri Lanka's Experience Transitioning from Gavi Support. LNCT and IHP.*

Source: Asian Development Bank assessment team.

(ii) Option 2: Third party logistics providers and direct delivery to health care institutions

Storage and distribution can be outsourced to or augmented by third party logistics providers (3PL) from the private sector that will use their distribution centers for storing and direct delivery to the health facilities based on agreed replenishment period, periodic consumption, minimum stock, and maximum stock.

In this configuration, MSD's role will be to conduct forecasting and supply planning, initiate procurement for framework agreements, monitor consumption and stock levels of the health facilities, advice 3PL quantities to replenish to the health facilities, and advice quantities to procure or supply in each call off under the framework agreements. Case Highlights 4 is an illustration.

Case Highlights 4: South Africa—Direct Delivery to Facilities

Background

South Africa faced challenges with fragmented supply chains, stockouts, and inefficiencies in delivering medicines to health care facilities. To address these issues, the government introduced framework agreements for procurement.

Approach

South Africa established framework agreements with suppliers, allowing direct delivery of medicines to health care facilities on short on-call basis. These agreements outline the terms, pricing, and quantities of medicines, simplifying the procurement process and ensuring a more efficient supply chain with reduced need for warehouse space and buffer stock.

Results

- ***Streamlined supply chain.*** Framework agreements have simplified the supply chain by eliminating intermediaries, reducing complexity, and ensuring direct delivery of medicines to health care facilities.
- ***Minimized stockouts.*** Direct delivery through framework agreements has minimized stockouts at health care facilities, ensuring that essential medicines are available when needed.
- ***Reduced warehouse operations.*** The direct delivery eliminated or reduced the need for warehousing, keeping buffer stocks by the government, and transporting the items to the facilities.

Source: Asian Development Bank assessment team.

(iii) Option 3: Fourth party logistics provider

Fourth-party logistics (4PL) is an operational model in which a business outsources its entire supply chain management and logistics to one external service provider. If MOH chooses this model, MOH can give a single contract to SPC or a 4PL to be responsible for uninterrupted supply of all the medicine needs on a continuous basis based on an approved list of selected products, an estimated range of quantities, agreed unit prices, and transportation and supply chain management cost. The 4PL can be paid periodically based on actual consumption of products and agreed transportation and supply chain management costs.

The 4PL or SPC will then be responsible for forecasting, supply planning, procuring, quality assurance, contracting 3PL, supplying (either by 3PL or through their own retail outlets), stock and consumption monitoring, and reporting. The role of MOH, in this configuration, will be to set technical standards through EML, National Drug Therapeutic Committee, and National Drug Formulary; prepare Annual Procurement List; employ pricing and market shaping strategies; contract and manage 4PL; conduct monitoring and evaluation; ensure rational use of medicines; and keep an oversight of the overall pharmaceutical supply chain management. Case Highlights 5 depicts this arrangement.

Case Highlights 5: Pharmaceutical Supply Chain Management in the People's Republic of China

The People's Republic of China does not have any central medical store. Managers of health facilities select medicines based on recommendations of clinicians, and the list is influenced by price of volume base procurement. Each individual health facility's manager quantifies the procurement requirements. For essential drugs and generic drugs with large consumption, the provincial government leads the centralized drug procurement and lists the medicines with reduced prices on a website for public health care institutions to complete the procurement process online. Generic drugs and commonly used low-cost drugs are purchased directly by hospitals. The drug supply directly flows from the manufacturer and/or supplier to the health facilities and then to the patients.

Each individual health facility is responsible for the procurement of medicines for their respective facility. There is no information flow to and from the health facility to the central level. Regarding rational prescribing, basically doctors follow their best knowledge gained from their medical education, but nowadays in the country, they are required to prescribe medicines procured through "volume based procurement."

Source: Asian Development Bank assessment team.

(iv) Option 4: E-procurement through central prequalification, price negotiation, and framework agreements with decentralized procurement through drug revolving fund

In this configuration, a competent unit at the central level (either MOH, MSD, SPC, or any other unit) pools the whole country demand for pharmaceuticals and medical products based on an approved list of selected products; prequalifies a range of suppliers and outlets; and publishes a catalogue of prequalified products, suppliers, outlets, and their unit prices for electronic procurement directly by the health facilities. Each prequalified supplier can have a minimum volume guarantee that they commit to sell over a period and the online catalogue will continuously monitor and update the quantity sold and quantities remaining from their volume guarantee to ensure that all prequalified suppliers receive minimum orders.

While the health facilities can directly choose products and place orders for selected products and quantities for direct delivery to the health facilities by prequalified suppliers through the online product catalog and e-procurement system, the central unit can settle the payments to the suppliers directly based on the framework agreements with them.

In this configuration, the role of MOH will be to set technical standards through EML, National Drug Therapeutic Committee, and National Drug Formulary; forecasting and demand pooling; employing strategic purchasing, pricing, and market-shaping strategies; prequalifying, contracting, and managing e-procurement suppliers; conducting monitoring and evaluation; ensuring rational use of medicines; providing technical assistance; and keeping an oversight of the overall pharmaceutical supply chain management. The e-procurement suppliers' role will be to monitor consumption and keep a minimum stock of listed items for ready supply; and report back the supply and consumption. The health facilities' role will be to forecast and share their annual consumptions based on an approved product list, monitor and manage their stock, place orders with the prequalified e-procurement supplier, and report back to the central level. Case Highlights 6 details an application in Indonesia.

Case Highlights 6: Indonesia's E-Katalog System

In 2011, Indonesia launched the E-Katalog system, a comprehensive e-procurement platform for pharmaceuticals. The system aimed to centralize the procurement process, increase competition among suppliers, and improve access to quality medicines and decentralize the ordering process. The E-Katalog platform provides real-time information on available pharmaceutical products, their prices, suppliers, and distribution details. It also enables health care facilities to place electronic orders and receive timely deliveries of essential medicines.

Supplier Registration

Pharmaceutical companies interested in supplying medicines to the government submit their products for registration on the E-Katalog platform. Suppliers are required to provide accurate product information, pricing, and quality assurance documents.

continued on next page

Case Highlights 6 *continued*

Quality Assurance

The E-Katalog system ensures that all registered products meet quality standards by requiring suppliers to submit relevant documentation, such as Good Manufacturing Practice certificates.

Results

- ***Efficiency:*** The E-Katalog system significantly streamlined the procurement process, reducing paperwork and administrative burdens.
- ***Transparency and accountability:*** The platform's transparency reduced the likelihood of corruption and fraud in the procurement process. Real-time price information and open bidding fostered fair competition.
- ***Cost savings:*** By promoting competition and reducing intermediary costs, the E-Katalog system contributed to cost savings for the government.
- ***Wider access to quality medicines:*** The system increased access to a wide range of quality-assured pharmaceutical products, benefiting health care facilities and patients.
- ***Digital transformation:*** The E-Katalog system marked a significant step in Indonesia's digital transformation journey, showcasing the government's commitment to modernizing public services.
- ***Scaling and expansion:*** The success of the E-Katalog system inspired Indonesia to expand its use beyond pharmaceuticals, encompassing other sectors of government procurement.

Source: Asian Development Bank assessment team.

6.4 Use of Data for Decision-Making

Conclusion 4: Apply data analytics

The pharmaceutical supply chain can benefit from the use of data analytics, effective monitoring and evaluation, and evidence-based decision-making practice to minimize the need for ad hoc and emergency decisions.

Inadequate utilization of end-use data analytics for timely and evidence-based decision-making contributes to the need for ad hoc and emergency decisions. There is a need to develop more user-friendly dashboards for SWASTHA and use data from SWASTHA for forecasting, supply planning, monitoring, and timely action. Currently, there are no information systems in use for product registration, pharmacovigilance, quality management system, and procurement.

Conclusion 5: Safeguard quality assurance and regulatory affairs

Scale up the capacity of quality assurance mechanism to effectively prevent the possibility of substandard and falsified medicines from entering the supply chain will protect public confidence on medicines available at government health facilities. Reducing registration lead time and regulatory barriers by adopting a reliance pathway that recognizes products registered by stringent regulatory authorities will encourage suppliers of high-quality products to enter the market for greater availability and competition.

Premarketing quality assurance in Sri Lanka is mostly dependent on product registration. Quality assurance during the procurement process lacks routinely applied prequalification and stringent quality checks. There is no comprehensive point-of-entry quality control mechanism.

There are shortages in the number of registered suppliers for many essential medical products. The lead time in product registration can be further reduced by following accelerated pathways that rely on processes conducted by other stringent regulatory authorities or WHO Listed Authorities to avoid redundant processes.

Conclusion 6: Develop human resources and capacity building

The lack of adequate human resources and trained professionals in the pharmaceutical supply chain is making it difficult to increase the efficiency of the supply chain in Sri Lanka.

The pharmaceutical supply chain has been suffering from the lack of adequate human resources and training, as institutional training courses on pharmaceutical supply chain are not available in Sri Lanka.

Conclusion 7: Establish a regional mechanism for market shaping and market-access

Strategic procurement practices, market shaping strategies, and use of framework agreements and pooled procurement mechanisms will reduce time, cost, and the vulnerability of Sri Lanka's public health pharmaceutical supply chain to market volatility.

Currently, Sri Lanka does not employ any strategic procurement and market shaping strategies. Due to small local market and lack of export of their pharmaceutical products, domestic manufacturers in Sri Lanka are facing challenges in achieving economies of scale, especially for the low-volume and high-unit-price products. Assuring consistently high quality of domestically manufactured products may need additional investments and the strengthening of the National Medicines Regulatory Authority. In the short term, quality assurance may come with price increases, but in the long run, assured quality may help the domestic manufacturers achieve economies of scale by being able to access the international market. There is also an untapped opportunity to set up an international or regional mechanism for multicountry quality assurance, market access, and pooled procurement.

Chapter 7

PROGRAM AND POLICY OPTIONS

Based on global best practices and different models of supply chain showcased in Chapter 6, it is believed that Sri Lanka would benefit from incorporating key features of other cases of pharmaceutical supply chain to address identified gaps. For example, by employing a decentralized e-procurement system such as the e-catalog and e-marketplace system adopted by Indonesia (E-Katalog of Indonesia), the role of MOH can be more focused on setting technical standards; conducting demand forecasting, prequalification, and price negotiation; formulating framework agreements with prequalified suppliers; and setting quantity caps for end users, while the role of end users would be to place and receive orders directly through the e-marketplace system.

Synthesizing the findings and analysis, seven pathways have been identified for further improvement and efficiency gain in Sri Lanka's pharmaceutical supply chain as presented in Figure 11.

Figure 11: Road Map to an Improved Pharmaceutical Supply Chain in Sri Lanka

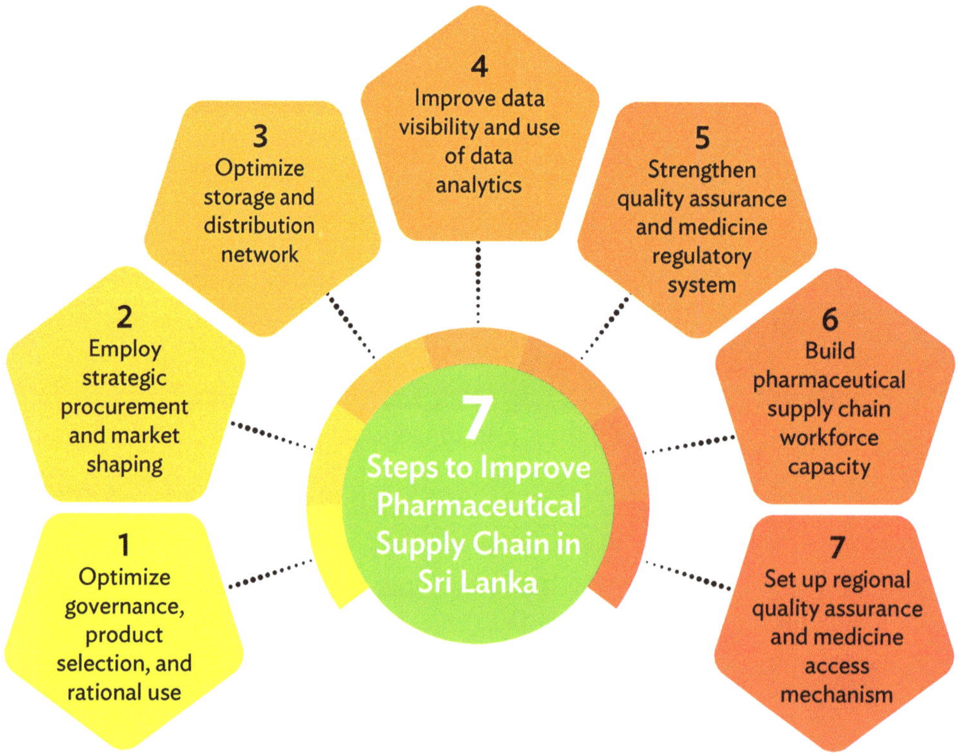

Source: Asian Development Bank assessment team.

7.1 Pathway 1: Governance, Rational Prescribing, and Product Selection

Enforcing national treatment guidelines, standard and simplified treatment protocols, EML, rational prescribing, and optimized product selection will result in reduced irrational prescriptions, reduced number of items to procure, higher administrative efficiency, and greater economies of scale saving significant health care costs. The short-term, medium-term, and long-term options for improving rational use of medicines and product selection are indicated in Box 6.

Box 6: Pathway 1—Options for Strengthening Pharmaceutical Supply Chain Governance

Short Term

- Review pharmaceutical supply chain governance structure and set up and/or strengthen necessary structures by clearly segregating technical standards setting, policy making, regulatory, market-shaping, procurement, logistics, and oversight roles with adequate coordination and accountability.
- Establish a technical unit (or units) within the Ministry of Health (MOH) that can take care of Health Technology Assessment, Essential Medicine List, National Treatment Guidelines, National Drug Therapeutic Committee, National Drug Formulary, Product Selection, and National Procurement List. The units need to be staffed by clinical, pharmaceutical, health economics, and public health experts. The units can host and be supported by the National Drug Therapeutic Committee, National Formulary Revision Committee, Health Technology Assessment team, and committees responsible for National Treatment Guidelines and National Procurement List. Alternatively, strengthen relevant committees within MOH with appropriate memberships, terms of reference, training, and tools.
- Regularly review and update National Treatment Guidelines and prepare simple treatment protocols to reduce the number of product variations within a therapeutic class. Disseminate the guidelines and protocols among treatment providers to ensure that the guidelines and protocols are followed both in the public and private sector. Organize clinical conferences to promote national treatment guidelines and encourage rational prescribing of medicines as per national treatment guidelines.
- Streamline and update the Essential Medicine List, National Formulary, and National Procurement List to select the absolute minimum number of products based on treatment guidelines, clinical rationale, pharmaco-economics, and cost effectiveness assessment for public procurement for maximum efficiency gain and to improve rational use.
- Establish a digitalized mechanism to efficiently review the prescriptions and when procuring named patient medicines.

Medium Term

- Strictly implement the generic prescription policies both in the public and private sectors to discourage prescribing brand names, brand preference, and brand dominance.
- Develop an electronic tool for standard practice in product selection and specifications that align with the National Treatment Guidelines, Essential Medicine List, National Drug Formulary, and Procurement Policy requirements (e.g. using international nonproprietary names).
- Introduce prescription and dispensing audit to enhance rational use of medicines. This can be done remotely by specialist teams by using electronic health records from SWASTHA and other health information systems.

continued on next page

Box 6 *continued*

Long Term

- Convert the committees and/or technical units within MOH that take care of Health Technology Assessment, Essential Medicine List, National Treatment Guidelines, National Drug Therapeutic Committee, National Drug Formulary, Product Selection, and National Procurement List into a National Institute of Clinical Excellence (modeled along the lines of the National Institute of Clinical Excellence in the United Kingdom) to perform these critical functions.
- Develop a periodic national survey plan to monitor the effectiveness of medicines and identify any drug resistance issue.

Source: Asian Development Bank assessment team.

7.2 Pathway 2: Strategic Procurement

Improving forecasting and supply planning, employing market shaping strategies, introducing framework agreements, and implementing strategic procurement practices could bridge the current gap between quantification and consumption; provide demand visibility to suppliers; ease the challenges with cash flow management; and reduce procurement lead time, administrative burdens, and prices. Box 7 contains options that can be considered to improve forecasting, supply planning, and strategic procurement.

Box 7: Pathway 2—Options to Employ Strategic Procurement

Short Term

- Conduct a data mapping, data availability assessment, and data cleaning exercise to access and use historical consumption data and identify data gaps.
- Develop and implement policies and standard operating procedures to conduct national forecasting and supply planning as a central level exercise based on data from the Medical Supply Management Information System and SWASTHA without burdening the health facilities to send estimations. Health facilities can only send requirements for forecast exceptional situations such as increased programmatic coverage, treatment campaigns, or additional satellite clinics. This can avoid considerable administrative burdens and staff time for compiling and sending information that is already available at the central level.
- Start conducting forecasting and supply planning based on the revised standard operating procedure, storage and distribution network, replenishment policy, need for buffer stocks, and procurement and supply cycles. Develop tools and train relevant staff on forecasting and supply planning.
- Clear all backlog payments to suppliers and repay debts to stabilize the pharmaceutical supply chain. Ensure timely and adequate budget allocations and disbursements to ensure predictable funding aligned to the procurement and supply chain cycles. Partial payments tied to staggered delivery and framework agreements can ease the cash flow.
- Integrate forecasting and supply planning modules within SWASTHA to support staff with data analytics for efficient forecasting and supply planning.

continued on next page

Box 7 *continued*

Medium Term

- Develop a comprehensive procurement strategy for different products and train relevant people on different procurement methods and instruments to implement the procurement strategies.
- Introduce framework and long-term procurement agreements with staggered delivery of variable quantities to reduce the procurement lead time and adjust to changing situations to avoid shortage or wastage.
- Develop and/or procure an enterprise resource planning system for procurement management (e.g., promise.lk) to be interoperable with SWASTHA for increased efficiency, information sharing, and coordination.
- Develop an electronic catalog and electronic procurement system for making prequalified products available for local and private sector procurement from prequalified suppliers at an agreed price. For example, for nonbulk purchases and purchasing of named patient items, prequalify a list of items and suppliers with agreed unit price and publish the list of prequalified items, suppliers, and unit prices from where the treatment facilities can directly procure items based on their needs. Although centrally prequalified for quality and negotiated for affordable prices, these items do not need to be procured and distributed centrally to reduce administrative burden and transaction costs.

Long Term

- Explore the feasibility of outsourcing the prequalification and due diligence process to a third party to identify and select suppliers for long-term framework agreements to reduce the burden on existing staff and to avoid interruptions to regular responsibilities.
- Transfer the administrative burden of procuring high-unit-price but low-volume products (e.g., cancer drugs and named patient drugs) to the market by identifying and preselecting retail facilities interested in carrying those medicines. In such cases, other than the government procuring, storing, and supplying the low-volume and high-cost medicines, the health facilities can order those medicines directly from the preselected retail suppliers based on actual need, and the government can reimburse the agreed cost directly to the retail supplier based on actual supply.

Source: Asian Development Bank assessment team.

7.3 Pathway 3: Optimized Distribution

Redesigning the distribution network by cutting the number of administrative steps and improving storage and distribution practices will reduce stock holding, transportation, and transaction costs; decrease the risks of quality loss; and improve availability of products. Box 8 presents actions that can be considered for warehousing, inventory management, and transportation.

Box 8: Options for Optimizing the Storage and Distribution Network

Short Term

- Undertake a distribution network analysis and distribution system optimization exercise to identify and set up optimum warehousing and delivery mechanisms. Consider direct delivery to the health facilities and reduce the number of tiers in the supply chain to reduce the administrative burden and stock keeping costs.
- Address the storage condition compliance issues at the health facilities by allocating sufficient space, procuring sturdy shelves and pallets, and installing temperature monitors, smoke detectors, and air conditioners.

Medium Term

- Set up inventory control and distribution policies considering replenishment period, minimum stock, maximum stock, safety stock, and buffer stock at various levels and for different products.
- Ensure that vacant staff positions for pharmaceutical supply management are filled, especially at the health facility level.
- Train relevant staff on inventory control, good storage practices, and good distribution practices.

Long Term

- Implement a redesigned distribution network based on options analysis and informed decision discussed in this section.

Source: Asian Development Bank assessment team.

7.4 Pathway 4: Data Visibility

Improved visibility and use of aggregated clinical and dispensing data and early warning systems will improve evidence-based decision making, stabilize the pharmaceutical supply chain system, and reduce product expiry and stockout. Box 9 shows some options to be considered.

Box 9: Options to Improve Data Visibility and Use Data Analytics

Short Term

- Fully develop, implement, and institutionalize SWASTHA for electronic health records, electronic logistics management information system, forecasting, monitoring and evaluation, and early warnings. This includes
    - o implementing SWASTHA in all health facilities, drugstores, and dispensing points;
    - o strengthening forecasting, warehouse management, and management dashboard modules of SWASTHA; and
    - o strengthening institutional arrangement and sustainability plan for full development, implementation, hosting, maintenance, and updating of SWASTHA.

continued on next page

Box 9 *continued*

- Train relevant staff, managers, and decision markers on using supply chain data and invest in evidence-based decision-making practices to establish a robust feedback loop for continuous improvement. Develop appropriate management dashboards and share actionable analysis for managers and policy makers for evidence-based decision making

Medium Term

- Procure, deploy, and roll out information systems for
  - o National Medicines Regulatory Authority especially for streamlining product registration;
  - o product selection and specification;
  - o procurement processing and management;
  - o e-catalog and e-procurement of prequalified products from prequalified suppliers at agreed prices;
  - o electronic system for quality assurance of medical products; and
  - o electronic system for pharmacovigilance reporting and causality assessment.
- Develop a road map for implementing Global Standards 1 (GS1) and barcode system for pharmaceutical products.
  GS1 is an international standards organization that manages the Global Trade Item Number system to identify companies and their products and services as used in Universal Product Code, European Article Numbering Code, and other barcodes; as well as in the electronic product codes for RFID tags. Implementation of a uniform barcode system based on GS1 will enhance data capturing at various points of the supply chain, reduce manual processes, and help in identifying potential falsified products.

Long Term

- Streamline parallel information systems and ensure interoperability of essential information systems for greater coordination.

Source: Asian Development Bank assessment team.

7.5 Pathway 5: Quality Assurance and Improved Medicine Regulatory System

Putting in place a proactive quality assurance system with adequate prevention and control mechanisms for premarketing and postmarketing quality assurance will reduce the incidence of quality-failed, substandard, and falsified products and improve the confidence in medicines available in the public sector. Streamlining the product registration system by introducing reliance and other accelerated registration pathways will reduce market access barriers, improve suppliers' availability and competition, and reduce costs. Options to consider are indicated in Box 10.

Box 10: Options to Strengthen Quality Assurance and Medicine Regulatory System

Short Term

- Strengthen the National Medicine Quality Assurance Laboratory (NMQAL) by hiring and training the required number of staff and developing a road map to be an ISO-certified laboratory and/or prequalified laboratory of the World Health Organization (WHO).
- Develop a more comprehensive national quality assurance strategy and implementation plan for guaranteeing the quality of medical products entering the market and public sector. The plan will have details on
  - o risk-based preventive measures and evidence-based correctives measures to minimize the possibility of substandard and falsified products entering the market;
  - o sampling methods to identify any quality failure at various levels of the supply chain;
  - o guidelines for prequalification for any pharmaceutical procurement that specify minimum quality standards as procurement eligibility, clarify requirements for certificate of quality and certificate of analysis issued by an accredited laboratory, and introduce a more comprehensive risk-based, point-of-entry quality check; and
  - o postqualification and imposition of hefty penalty and legal actions for supplying substandard and falsified products.
- Develop a policy and/or scheme for therapeutic items with inadequate number of registered products to encourage suppliers to register corresponding products that increase availability, options, and competition in procurement.

Medium Term

- Set up a national network of collaborative quality assurance laboratories with NMQAL taking the national reference laboratory and leadership role.
- Introduce a risk-based, point-of-entry testing mechanism or Global Standards 1 (GS1) practice to stop substandard, falsified, and noncompliant items from entering the country.
- Strengthen the quality assurance laboratory of the State Pharmaceutical Corporation to ensure premarketing quality assurance.

Long Term

- Leverage the WHO collaborative laboratory network for information exchange and outsource quality testing tasks to the network members as appropriate.
- Conduct a business process optimization review of the current procedures of the National Medicines Regulatory Authority (NMRA) to streamline processes, avoid redundancy, and address unnecessary dependency.
- Harmonize the common technical dossier used by NMRA with that of the International Council on Harmonization for registration of pharmaceuticals and the Association of Southeast Asian Nations common technical dossier format.
- Optimize and diversify the current processes for product registration by utilizing accelerated and reliance pathways and introducing differentiated pathways for product registration based on quality, safety, and efficacy risks.

Source: Asian Development Bank assessment team.

7.6 Pathway 6: Capacity Building

Enhancing the capacity of the pharmaceutical supply chain workforce and leadership will increase the overall efficiency and effectiveness of the public health pharmaceutical supply chain. The options in Box 11 can be considered for improving human resources for pharmaceutical supply chain management.

Box 11: Options to Build Pharmaceutical Supply Chain Workforce Capacity

Short Term

- Orient key leaders, policy makers, and managers on pharmaceutical systems strengthening and overview of pharmaceutical supply chain management.
- Conduct a pharmaceutical supply chain workforce assessment and develop a comprehensive pharmaceutical workforce development plan as part of a comprehensive human resources for health plan considering the functions, organograms, positions, job descriptions, and skills sets required at all levels of the pharmaceutical supply chain.
- Develop training courses and make preservice and in-service training arrangements for the pharmaceutical supply chain workforce. Priority in-service training courses may include:
  - overview of national pharmaceutical systems strengthening: goal, processes, organization, and stakeholders;
  - Essential Medicine List and product selection;
  - product registration: objectives, process, and pathways;
  - forecasting and supply planning;
  - procurement strategies and instruments for strategic purchasing;
  - good storage practices;
  - inventory management;
  - warehouse and distribution network and good distribution practices;
  - rational use of medicines;
  - pharmacovigilance;
  - price regulation;
  - drug resistance monitoring;
  - ageing, gender, and climate change issues in pharmaceutical supply chain;
  - monitoring, evaluation, and evidence-based decision making in pharmaceutical supply chain; and
  - quality assurance in pharmaceutical supply chain.

Medium Term

- Implement the pharmaceutical supply chain workforce development plan as part of the comprehensive human resources for health plan by filling in the vacant positions and training people appropriately.

Long Term

- Develop an online training platform for in-service training on pharmaceutical supply chain.
- Introduce pharmaceutical supply chain management courses in appropriate pre-service academic programs

Source: Asian Development Bank assessment team.

7.7 Pathway 7: Regional Medicines Access

In order to access international markets and achieve economies of scale, domestic manufacturers of medical products in Sri Lanka will need to achieve consistent quality assurance. The country needs to enhance the capacity of NMRA to gain international confidence in NMRA's quality assurance process. The varying market sizes, domestic manufacturing capacities, and quality assurance capabilities of national medicine regulatory authorities in Asia create the opportunity for setting up a multicountry collaborative mechanism. This mechanism will aim for harmonization and collective quality assurance and quality improvement, demand pooling, enhanced market access by addressing regulatory barriers, and conducting pooled procurement for greater predictability and economies of scale. It will also improve the capacity of domestic manufacturers, ensure quality of their products, and give them opportunities to export their products beyond local markets through quality assurance and market access activities. For participating countries, the mechanism will create opportunities for increased availability of products both domestically and internationally at lower prices through demand aggregation and economies of scale. Box 12 explores options.

Box 12: Options for Exploring Opportunities to Set Up a Regional Mechanism for Greater Medicine Access

Short Term

- Conduct a feasibility study for Sri Lanka to set up or take part in a regional and/or international quality assurance, market access, and pooled procurement mechanism.

Medium Term

- Set up a commission and/or unit under the Ministry of Health with persons who have relevant skill sets in employing price negotiation, market-shaping, and pricing strategies. This unit or commission can employ market-shaping and pricing strategies, prequalify products and suppliers, and establish framework agreements with prequalified suppliers. The State Pharmaceutical Corporation can then execute the procurement from the list of prequalified suppliers with framework agreements.
- Initiate setting up or taking part in a regional and/or international quality assurance, market access, and pooled procurement mechanism.

Long Term

- Harmonize Sri Lanka's regulatory and procurement practices with applicable global normative standards and internationally accepted principles and practices.

Source: Asian Development Bank assessment team.

APPENDIXES

Appendix 1: Methodology and Questionnaire Resource Pack

Appendix 1.1 Patient Interview Questionnaire—Pharmaceutical Services Satisfaction

To the enumerator: Please explain the following to the respondents and encode their responses in the tick boxes and blanks as briefly but completely as possible.

Introduction

The Ministry of Health is conducting an assessment of the National Pharmaceutical Supply Chain funded by the Asian Development Bank (ADB), to ensure that patient needs are met appropriately and effectively. Thank you for participating in this interview to support this assessment. Your feedback is important in helping us understand your experiences and perceptions of the pharmaceutical services provided at public health facilities. Your responses will contribute to improving the quality of health care services in Sri Lanka.

Section 1: Demographic Information

Gender : [ ] Male [ ] Female
Age : ____________________
Educational Level : [ ] Primary School [ ] Secondary School [ ] University
[ ] Other (please specify) ____________________
Name of the Health Facility : ____________________
Type of Patient : [ ] Out-Patient [ ] Clinic Patient [ ] In-ward Patient [ ] Other

Section 2: Pharmaceutical Services Satisfaction

1. On a scale of 1 to 10, how satisfied are you with the overall pharmaceutical services you received at this health facility? (1 being very dissatisfied and 10 being very satisfied) ____________________

2. Were the prescribed medicines readily available at the facility's pharmacy during your visit?
[ ] Yes [ ] No

3. 3. Did the health care staff provide clear instructions on how to take your medications?
[ ] Yes [ ] No

4. How would you rate the cleanliness and organization of the pharmacy or medication dispensing area?
   [ ] Very Clean [ ] Moderately Clean [ ] Not Clean

5. Did you experience any delays in receiving your medications? If yes, please describe.
   [ ] Yes [ ] No
   Describe: ____________________

6. Were you provided with information about potential side effects or interactions of your medications?
   [ ] Yes [ ] No

7. Did you find the pharmacy staff to be courteous and helpful in addressing your concerns or questions?
   [ ] Yes [ ] No

8. Did you encounter any issues with the packaging or labeling of your medications?
   [ ] Yes [ ] No

9. Did you receive any counseling or education regarding the proper use of your medications?
   [ ] Yes [ ] No

10. On a scale of 1 to 10, how would you rate the overall convenience of obtaining your medications at this health facility? (1 being very inconvenient and 10 being very convenient)
    ____

Section 3: Additional Feedback

1. Were there any specific challenges or positive aspects of your experience with pharmaceutical services that you would like to highlight? ____________________
   ____
   ____

2. Do you have any suggestions for improving pharmaceutical services at this health facility?
   ____
   ____

Section 4: Consent and Contact Information

Your participation in this interview is voluntary. Your responses will be kept confidential and used only for research purposes. If you are willing to be contacted for follow-up discussions, please provide your contact information. ____________________

Name (optional) : ____________________

Phone Number (optional): ____________________

Thank you for taking the time to participate in this survey. Your input is greatly appreciated and will contribute to enhancing pharmaceutical services in public health facilities.

Appendix 1.2: Facility Assessment Questionnaire

To the enumerator: Please explain the following to the respondents and encode their responses in the tick boxes and blanks as briefly but completely as possible.

Facility Level Indicators to be Assessed

1. Proportion of health facilities that have a core set of relevant essential medicines available and affordable on a sustainable basis
2. Proportion of pharmaceutical supply chain positions that are filled in with licensed pharmacists, pharmacy technicians, or pharmacy assistants
3. Out-of-pocket expenditure out of total pharmaceutical expenditure at various levels of service delivery
4. Percent of product losses by value due to expired medicines, damage, or theft per value received
5. Mean percentage variation between the forecast and actual consumption for a set of tracer products
6. Percent of median international price paid for a set of tracer medicines that was part of the last regular Ministry of Health procurement (disaggregated by three types of procurement: regular procurement, local procurement, and emergency procurement)
7. Percent of supplier with on-time and in full delivery (disaggregated by three types of procurement: regular procurement, local procurement, and emergency procurement)
8. Percent of orders received on time and in full (OTIF)
9. Percent of medicines prescribed according to National Treatment Guidelines
10. Percent of pharmaceutical wastes disposed according to the appropriate guidelines

Pharmaceutical Supply Chain Assessment: Self Reporting Questionnaire for Health Facilities

Introduction

This checklist is designed to guide the assessment of pharmaceutical supply chain facilities within the framework of the Pharmaceutical Supply Chain Assessment in Sri Lanka. The purpose of this assessment is to evaluate the maturity and effectiveness of the pharmaceutical supply chain operations. Thank you for completing this assessment for your facility.

Facility Information

Facility Name : ______________________________

Location
(District and Province) : ______________________________

Type of Health Facility
(Regional Medical Supply Division/Teaching Hospital/Specialized Hospital/Provincial General Hospital/District General Hospital/Base Hospital Type A/Base Hospital Type B/Divisional Hospital Type A/Divisional Hospital Type B/Divisional Hospital Type C/ Primary Medical Care Unit):

____

____

Contact Person
(Name and Position) : ______________________________

1. Are all essential medicines that need to be always available at your facility currently available in your stock?
   [ ] Yes [ ] No

   1a. Total number of essential medicines that need to be always available at your facility
   (Please enter number of medicine items) ______________________________

   1b. Total number of essential medicines that are currently available in your stock
   (Please enter number of medicine items) ______________________________

2. What number of essential medicines did your facility experience stock-outs over the past one year?
   (Please enter the number) ______________________________

3. What are the different staff categories used in your facility? (Please list all categories)

   ____

   ____

4a. What is the total number of pharmaceutical supply chain management related positions approved for your facility? ______________________________

4b. How many of these pharmaceutical supply chain management related positions at your facility are currently vacant? ______________________________

5. How many of these pharmaceutical supply chain management related positions at your facility are currently filled in by a Licensed Pharmacist, Pharmacy Technician, or a Pharmacy Assistant?

   ____

6. What percentage of prescribed medicines at your facility did the patients need to buy through out-of-pocket expenditure over the past one year? (Please provide an estimated percentage)
____

7. What percentage of total pharmaceutical products at your facility was lost due to expired medicines, damage, or theft over the past one year? (Please provide an estimated percentage in quantity and in monetary value) _______________

8. What was the mean percentage of variation between annual forecasted and actual consumption of the top 10 essential medicines in your facility over the past one year? (Please provide a percentage)
____

9. Did your facility make any local procurement of medicines over the past one year?
[] Yes [] No
(If no, please skip questions 12 and 13 and go to question 14)

10. If yes, please name the item procured and their unit prices paid.

Sl.	Item Procured	Unit Price (SLR)	Unit
Example	Thyroxine 50 mcg	4.00	Per tablet
1.			
2.			
3.			
4.			
5.			

11. If your facility conducted local procurement over the past one year, how many suppliers got a purchase order and how many of the suppliers delivered pharmaceutical products on time and in full as per your purchase order?
Total number of suppliers that received a purchased order: _______________
Number of suppliers that delivered on time and in full: _______________

12. How many order requests for pharmaceutical products did your facility submit to Medical Supply Division/Regional Medical Supply Division over the past one year? How many of requested orders were received by your facility from MSD/RMSD on time and in full over the past one year?
Total number of orders requested: _______________
Number of orders received on time and in full: _______________

13. What percentage of medicines prescribed in your facility adhere to the National Treatment Guidelines? (Please provide a percentage) ____________________

14. Does your facility dispose of pharmaceutical waste according to the standard protocols? Please describe.
    [ ] Yes [ ] No
    Please describe how pharmaceutical wastes are disposed of in your facility:
    ____
    ____
    ____

Additional comments: Challenges and suggestions for improving pharmaceutical supply chain
____
____
____

Thank you for participating in this assessment. Your input is valuable for improving pharmaceutical supply chain management in Sri Lanka.

Appendix 1.3: Pharmaceutical Store Assessment Checklist

To the enumerator: Please explain the following to the respondents and encode their responses in the tick boxes and blanks as briefly but completely as possible.

Name of Facility : ____________________

Facility Type
(RMSD/TH/Specialized Hospital/PGH/DGH/BH A/BH B/DHA/DHB/DH C/PMCU)
____
____

Location : ____________________
Date of Assessment : ____________________
Assessor Name : ____________________

	Ideal Practice	Observation			
		Fully Practiced	Partially Practiced	Not Practiced	Not Applicable/ Remark
1	The facility has designated areas for reception zone, inspection zone, packing and delivery preparation zone, storage area, delivery zone, and office area				
2	Storage area is secured with a lock and key, and is accessible during normal working hours with access limited to authorized personnel				
3	Store area has sufficient space for storing and organizing different products for easy access, inspection, and counting. The current space and organization is sufficient for existing products and reasonable expansion (i.e., receipt of expected product deliveries for foreseeable future).				
4	The storeroom is maintained in good condition (clean, all trash removed, sturdy shelves, organized boxes). Storeroom is cleaned and disinfected regularly. Storage area is visually free from harmful insects and rodents (there are no traces of droppings of rodents or insects).				
5	Storeroom is secured from the risk of water penetration and high humidity at all times of the day and during all seasons				
6	Smoke detector, fire alarm, and fire safety equipment are available and easily accessible in the storeroom and personnel are trained to use them				

continued on next page

Table *continued*

	Ideal Practice	Observation			
		Fully Practiced	Partially Practiced	Not Practiced	Not Applicable/ Remark
7	Products are stored on pallets or shelves in a dry, well-lit, well-ventilated condition out of direct sunlight				
8	Cartons are stacked at least 10 centimeters (cm) (4 inches) off the floor, 30 cm (1 foot) away from the walls and other stacks, and not more than 2.5 meters (8 feet) high				
9	The facility maintains cold storage for vaccines, drugs, and commodities that require it				
10	The storeroom temperature is controlled and monitored regularly with sufficient air-conditioning, thermometers, and temperature chart				
11	Medical supplies are stored away from insecticides, chemicals, old files, office supplies, and other materials				
12	Condoms and other latex products are stored away from electric motors and fluorescent lights				
13	The facility keeps narcotics and other controlled substances in a locked place				
14	The facility stores flammable products separately from other products and takes appropriate safety precautions for them				
15	The facility separates damaged and expired products from the regular stock and disposes them as per guidelines				
16	The facility uses location codes and shelf labels for easy allocation and management of storage location for products				
17	There are bin cards attached to the stack of products. Cartons are arranged so that arrows point up and identification labels, expiry dates, and manufacturing dates are clearly visible				
18	The facility rotates the supply, organizes stock and dispenses products on a first expiry first out manner				
19	The facility has a policy for minimum and maximum stock of a product to prevent stock out or over stock				

continued on next page

Table *continued*

	Ideal Practice	Observation			
		Fully Practiced	Partially Practiced	Not Practiced	Not Applicable/ Remark
20	The facility maintains stock cards, inventory movement records (for receipt, registration and storage, and dispatch of products), and produces periodic warehouse reports and/or inventory reports				
21	The facility makes it a practice to conduct sample stock count, spot count, and full stock count on a periodic basis				
22	The facility uses a warehouse management information system or logistic management information system				
23	The facility minimizes the risk of loss of quality of products during transportation to other facilities and/or end users by ensuring that the products are transported under ideal temperatures, free from direct sunlight and water				
24	The facility conducts periodic stock analysis by using previous distribution data to calculate average monthly consumption and forecast current stock level				
25	Staff in charge of the store have clearly assigned job description and are trained on storage, distribution, and inventory management				

Scoring Scale

Fully practiced	:	2
Partially practiced	:	1
Not practiced	:	0
Total score	:	Add all the scores against each criteria

Percentage of Compliance

(Total score obtained by a facility) + (50 – 2* no. of not applicable cases) × 100

Appendix 1.4.1: Data Collection Method for National-Level Indicators

	Indicator	Data Collection Method
1	Proportion of health facilities that have a core set of relevant essential medicines available and affordable on a sustainable basis	• Check historical and migrated data on SWASTHA, the integrated electronic health records and logistics management information system introduced in 2023. • Triangulate the findings with facility assessment data.
2	Percentage of products on Essential Medicines List (EML) that are currently manufactured or co-manufactured within the country	• Collect data from regulatory authorities or relevant government agencies regarding the list of medicines on the EML, number of medicines registered on the EML and their manufacturing origin (domestic or imported). • Conduct an analysis of private sector capacity, challenges, government policies, and opportunities for public–private fit.
3	Technical efficiency of the current pharmaceutical supply chain system as a percentage of current efficiency over optimum efficiency	• This indicator is a measure of how well the existing pharmaceutical supply chain system is performing compared to its optimal potential. It is calculated using Data Envelopment Analysis (DEA), a method commonly used to assess the relative efficiency of decision-making units (in this case, pharmaceutical supply chain systems) when there are multiple inputs and outputs involved. • Suggested inputs: (i) financial resources: total budget allocated to the pharmaceutical supply chain; (ii) human resources: number of staff involved in procurement, distribution, and monitoring; (iii) infrastructure: warehouse capacity, transportation facilities, technology. • Suggested outputs: (i) timely delivery of medicines: percentage of medicines delivered on time; (ii) inventory management: percentage of optimal inventory levels maintained; (iii) reduction in wastage: percentage reduction in expired or wasted medicines; and (iv) quality assurance: percentage of medicines meeting quality standards. • Data collected for the above inputs and outputs will be normalized by dividing them with the highest value for each item and then efficiency scores will be calculated using the DEA model.
4	Index to assess the relevance and appropriateness of the current pharmaceutical procurement guidelines in meeting the specific needs and challenges of the health care system	• Collect and review current laws, policies, and guidelines related to pharmaceutical procurement. • Work with State Pharmaceutical Company and Medical Supply Division to complete the World Health Organization model quality assurance system tool.
5	Average number of days for decision making on a medicine application for registration	• Gather data from the regulatory authority responsible for medicine registration on the average time taken to review and approve medicine registration applications for the last 10 cases. • Conduct focus group discussions with registration applicants.
6	Proportion of pharmaceutical supply chain positions that are filled in with licensed pharmacists, pharmacy technicians, or pharmacy assistants	• Collect and review data from Human Resources for Health report and database at the central level for the whole country. • Triangulate findings with the facility assessment results.
7	Data on safety, efficacy, and cost effectiveness of medicines available and used to inform essential medicines selection	• In-depth interview with the unit responsible for EML. • Review official records, reports, and data from regulatory bodies, health agencies, and relevant research studies to assess the availability and use of data for essential medicines selection.

	Indicator	Data Collection Method
8	Out-of-pocket expenditure out of total pharmaceutical expenditure at various levels of service delivery	• Obtain and review secondary information including other surveys, if available. • Triangulate the findings with facility assessment results. • Conduct an analysis of central level data for utilization of domestic and donor funding for pharmaceutical procurement.
9	Percentage of households more than 20 kilometers away from a dispensing facility or pharmacy	• Use geographic information systems data and population data to calculate the percentage of households that are more than 20 kilometers away from dispensing facilities or pharmacies. • Use secondary information, if available.
10	Percentage of product losses by value due to expired medicines or damage or theft per value received	• Collect data from pharmaceutical supply chain management records, inventory management systems, and official reports to calculate the percentage of product losses by value. • Triangulate information with facility level assessment data for the same indicator.
11	Existence of an EML published within the past five years	• Review official documents, policy statements, and publications to confirm the existence of a national EML published within the past five years.
12	Percentage of medicines selected from EML over the total number of medicines procured	• Collect procurement data from relevant government departments and agencies to calculate the percentage of medicines procured from the EML.
13	Mean percentage of variation between the forecast and actual consumption for a set of tracer products	• Analyze consumption data and forecasts from health facilities to calculate the mean percentage variation. • Triangulate findings with the results from facility assessments.
14	Percentage of median international price paid for a set of tracer medicines that was part of the last regular MOH procurement (disaggregated by three types of procurement: regular procurement, local procurement, and emergency procurement)	• Obtain procurement data and international price data to calculate the percentage of the median international price paid for selected medicines. • Use facility assessment data for local procurements.
15	Percentage of supplier with on-time and in full delivery (disaggregated by three types of procurement: regular procurement, local procurement, and emergency procurement)	• Collect supplier performance data from SPC and MSD and evaluate the percentage of on-time and complete deliveries. • Use facility assessment data for local procurements. • Conduct a review of prequalification and postqualification process at the central level.
16	Percentage of temperature-controlled vehicles in the total distribution fleet	• Review data from distribution and logistics unis of MSD to calculate the percentage of temperature-controlled vehicles in the fleet.
17	Percentage of samples tested that failed quality control testing	• Obtain quality control testing data from regulatory authorities or quality control laboratories to calculate the percentage of samples that failed testing in the past one year.
18	Percentage of availability of National Treatment Guidelines that have been reviewed or updated within the last three years	• Review the National Treatment Guidelines and associated documents for the tracer products to determine the percentage of guidelines that have been reviewed or updated within the specified timeframe.
19	Percentage of recorded adverse event reports that are assessed for causality	• Collect adverse event reporting data and assess the percentage of recorded reports that have been evaluated for causality over the past one year

continued on next page

Table *continued*

	Indicator	Data Collection Method
20	Percentage of key action items implemented from the National Action Plan on Antimicrobial Resistance (AMR)	• Review official documents and policy reports to determine the availability and implementation status of the action plan on AMR containment. • Conduct key informant interviews with the unit responsible for AMR.
21	Percentage of health facilities that submit complete logistics management information system (LMIS) reports on time to their reporting unit	• Collect LMIS data and calculate the percentage of health facilities that submit complete reports on time.
22	Existence of a policy or strategy that sets standards for collection and management of pharmaceutical supply chain information for monitoring and evaluation	• Ask MSD and review official policy documents and relevant publications (e.g., monitoring and evaluation plan) to determine the existence of a policy or strategy related to pharmaceutical supply chain information collection and management.

Appendix 1.4.2: Suitability Index Assessment for Pharmaceutical Procurement Guidelines

To the enumerator: Please explain the following to the respondents and encode their responses in the tick boxes and blanks as briefly but completely as possible.

Instructions

This tool aims to evaluate the comprehensiveness and suitability of the current pharmaceutical procurement guidelines in meeting the specific needs and challenges of the health care system in Sri Lanka. Please assign a score for each criterion and calculate the final suitability index percentage.

Scoring Scale

Fully addressed : 3
Adequately addressed : 2
Partially addressed : 1
Not addressed : 0

	Criteria	Question	Maximum Score	Obtained Score
1	Alignment with international best practices	How well do the guidelines align with internationally recognized best practices for pharmaceutical procurement?	3	
2	Responsiveness to local context	To what extent do the guidelines take into account the unique challenges and characteristics of the local health care system?	3	
3	Clarity of procedures	How clear and well-defined are the procurement procedures outlined in the guidelines?	3	
4	Inclusion of sustainable procurement principles	Do the guidelines incorporate principles of sustainability, including environmental, social, and economic considerations?	3	
5	Consideration of public health needs	How effectively do the guidelines address the procurement of essential medicines and medical products that are critical to public health?	3	
6	Adaptability to changing circumstances	How flexible are the guidelines in adapting to changing health care demands, technological advancements, and unforeseen disruptions?	3	
		TOTAL	**18**	

Calculation of Suitability Index

Sum up the scores assigned to each criterion.
Divide the total score by the maximum possible score (18) and multiply by 100 to get the suitability index percentage.

Appendix 1.5: Key Informant Interview Questionnaire

To the enumerator: Please explain the following to the respondents and encode their responses in the tick boxes and blanks as briefly but completely as possible.

Introduction

Thank you for participating in this interview. The information you provide will be valuable for assessing the pharmaceutical supply chain in Sri Lanka. Your insights will contribute to a better understanding of the current situation and potential areas for improvement. All information shared will be treated confidentially.

Section 1: General Information

Name of Interviewee : ______________________________
Designation and Organization: ______________________________
Contact Information : ______________________________

Section 2: Indicator-Specific Questions

Indicator 1: Percentage of products on EML that are currently manufactured or co-manufactured within the country

1. Could you provide information about the proportion of products on the Essential Medicines List (EML) that are currently manufactured or co-manufactured within the country?
   ____
   ____
   ____

2. Are there any government policies or incentives in place to promote local manufacturing of essential medicines?
   [ ] Yes [ ] No

Indicator 2: Presence of a National Medicines Policy implementation plan (or pharmaceutical sector strategic plan) that sets activities, responsibilities, budget, and timeline

3. Is there a National Medicines Policy implementation plan or a pharmaceutical sector strategic plan in place?
   [ ] Yes [ ] No

Indicator 3: Average number of days for decision making on a medicine application for registration

4. Could you provide information on the average number of days it takes for the regulatory authority to make a decision on a medicine application for registration? ______________________________
   ____

5. Are there any initiatives or strategies in place to streamline the registration process and reduce decision-making time?
   [ ] Yes [ ] No

Indicator 4: Data on safety, efficacy, and cost-effectiveness of medicines available and used to inform essential medicines selection

6. How does the country gather data on the safety, efficacy, and cost-effectiveness of medicines to inform essential medicines selection? ______________________________
   ____
   ____
   ____

7. Are there established mechanisms to ensure that only medicines meeting these criteria are included in the Essential Medicines List?
   [ ] Yes [ ] No

Indicator 5: Total expenditure on pharmaceuticals as a percent of total expenditure on health

8. What is the current total expenditure on pharmaceuticals as a percentage of the total health expenditure in the country? ______________________________
   ____

9. Are there any efforts to manage and optimize pharmaceutical expenditure without compromising health care quality?
   [ ] Yes [ ] No

Indicator 6: Percentage of households more than 20 kilometers away from a dispensing facility or pharmacy

10. Can you provide insights into the percentage of households that are located more than 20 kilometers away from a dispensing facility or pharmacy?
    ____
    ____
    ____

11. Are there plans to improve access to health care facilities, especially in remote areas?
    [ ] Yes [ ] No

Indicator 7: Percentage of product losses by value due to expired medicines or damage or theft per value received

12. What is the percentage of product losses by value due to expired medicines, damage, or theft in the pharmaceutical supply chain? ______________________________
    ____

13. Are there strategies or measures in place to minimize product losses and enhance supply chain security?
    [ ] Yes [ ] No

Indicator 8: Percentage of medicines selected from EML over the total number of medicines procured

14. What percentage of medicines procured by the government are selected from the Essential Medicines List? ____________________

15. Is there a mechanism to ensure that procurement aligns with the EML to improve medicine availability?
    [ ] Yes [ ] No

Indicator 9: Mean percentage of variation between the forecast and actual consumption for a set of tracer products

16. Could you provide insights into the average percentage of variation between forecasted and actual consumption for selected tracer products? ____________________

17. Are there initiatives to enhance forecasting accuracy and minimize discrepancies?
    [ ] Yes [ ] No

Indicator 10: Percentage of median international price paid for a set of tracer medicines that was part of the last regular Ministry of Health procurement

18. Are there strategies to ensure cost-effective procurement while maintaining medicine quality?
    [ ] Yes [ ] No

Indicator 11: Availability of National Action Plan on the containment of antimicrobial resistance reviewed or updated within the last two years

19. Is there a National Action Plan on the containment of antimicrobial resistance in place?
    [ ] Yes [ ] No

20. How frequently is the National Action Plan reviewed and updated to address evolving challenges?
    ____

Indicator 12: Existence of a policy or strategy that sets standards for collection and management of pharmaceutical supply chain information for monitoring and evaluation

21. Is there a policy or strategy that outlines standards for the collection and management of pharmaceutical supply chain information?
    [ ] Yes [ ] No

Conclusion

Thank you for sharing your insights. Your input is valuable for the assessment process. If there's anything else you would like to add or any additional information you believe is important, please feel free to do so. ____________________

____

____

Contact Information

If there are any follow-up questions or clarifications needed, please provide your preferred contact details. ____________________

____

____

Appendix 1.6: Expert Interview Questionnaire—System Design Insights for Pharmaceutical Supply Chain Improvement

To the enumerator: Please explain the following to the respondents and encode their responses in the tick boxes and blanks as briefly but completely as possible.

Introduction

Thank you for participating in this interview. Your expertise is invaluable for shaping the future of the pharmaceutical supply chain in Sri Lanka. Your insights will help identify strategies for enhancing various aspects of the system design. All information shared will be treated confidentially.

Section 1: General Information

Name of Interviewee : ______________________________
Designation and Organization: ______________________________
Contact Information : ______________________________

Section 2: Insights for System Design Improvement

Area 1: Domestic manufacturing and efficient registration

1. In your opinion, how can the domestic manufacturing of essential medicines be encouraged and improved to ensure availability and reduce dependence on imports? ______________________________
____
____
____

2. What strategies or reforms could expedite and streamline the registration process for pharmaceutical products while maintaining rigorous quality standards? ______________________________
____
____
____

Area 2: Improving forecasting accuracy

3. What methods or practices can enhance forecasting accuracy for pharmaceutical product demand?
____
____
____
____

4. Are there any technologies or data analytics tools that can be leveraged?
[ ] Yes [ ] No

Area 3: Strategic procurement and delivery mechanisms

5. How can strategic procurement be established to ensure cost-effectiveness and timely availability of pharmaceuticals? ____

6. Are framework agreements and direct delivery mechanisms feasible options for Sri Lanka?
   [ ] Yes [ ] No

7. What key factors should be considered in designing a direct delivery system to health care facilities?
   ____

Area 4: Reducing warehousing levels and buffer stock requirements

8. What role can third-party logistics (3PL) or fourth-party logistics (4PL) play in reducing warehousing levels and buffer stock requirements? ____

9. Are there any challenges to be addressed?
   [ ] Yes [ ] No

Area 5: Improving visibility of supply chain

10. What technological solutions or tools can be employed to enhance visibility across different levels of the pharmaceutical supply chain? ____

11. How can real-time information sharing be optimized? ____

Area 6: Ensuring appropriate use of medical products

12. How can appropriate use of medical products be ensured to prevent overuse, underuse, or misuse?

13. Are there strategies for promoting rational prescribing and dispensing practices?
    [ ] Yes [ ] No

Area 7: Improving monitoring and evaluation

14. What methods or approaches can enhance monitoring and evaluation of the pharmaceutical supply chain?

15. How can performance indicators be effectively measured and analyzed?

Area 8: Ensuring necessary supply chain workforce

16. What steps can be taken to ensure an adequate and skilled supply chain workforce, including pharmacists, pharmacy technicians, and logistics professionals?

Area 9: Improving communication and coordination among stakeholders

17. How can communication and coordination among stakeholders in the pharmaceutical supply chain be improved?

18. Are there platforms or mechanisms for effective collaboration?
    [ ] Yes [ ] No

Conclusion

Your insights are invaluable for shaping a more efficient and effective pharmaceutical supply chain system. If there's any additional information or innovative ideas you would like to contribute, please feel free to share. ____________________

____

____

____

Contact Information

If there are any follow-up questions or clarifications needed, please provide your preferred contact details. ____________________

Appendix 1.7: Focus Group Discussion Questions—Improving Pharmaceutical Supply Chain Robustness, Agility, and Visibility

To the enumerator: Please explain the following to the respondents and encode their responses in the tick boxes and blanks as briefly but completely as possible.

Introduction

Thank you for joining this focus group discussion. Your valuable insights will help identify strategies for enhancing the pharmaceutical supply chain to ensure access to appropriate medical products for all Sri Lankans in a cost-effective manner.

Section 1: Understanding Challenges and Needs

1. What challenges or barriers have you observed or experienced in accessing medical products through the current pharmaceutical supply chain? ______________________________
____
____
____

2. In your opinion, what aspects of the supply chain need improvement to ensure that medical products are available when needed and used appropriately? ______________________________
____
____
____

Section 2: Improving Robustness and Agility

1. What measures can be taken to enhance the robustness of the pharmaceutical supply chain, making it resilient to disruptions such as disasters, emergencies, or supply shortages?
____
____
____
____

2. How can the supply chain be made more agile to quickly adapt to changes in demand, emerging health concerns, or new medical products entering the market? ______________________________
____
____
____

Section 3: Enhancing Visibility

1. How can visibility across the supply chain be improved to ensure better tracking of medical products from manufacturer to end-user? ______

2. What technological solutions or approaches can facilitate this? ______

Section 4: Cost-Effectiveness and Access

1. How can the supply chain be optimized to ensure access to appropriate medical products while keeping costs in check? ______

2. Are there ways to reduce wastage, overstocking, or underutilization of products?
   [ ] Yes   [ ] No

Section 5: Promoting Appropriate Use of Medical Products

1. What strategies can be employed to ensure that medical products are used appropriately according to guidelines and patient needs? ______

2. How can rational prescribing and dispensing be promoted? ______

Conclusion

Your insights are invaluable in shaping a pharmaceutical supply chain that meets the needs of the population efficiently and effectively. If you have any additional thoughts, ideas, or suggestions, please feel free to share. ______

Appendix 1.8: List of Tracer Products

Vital Pharmaceuticals (13)

SRNO	Item Description	VEN	ABC	Item Class	Unit Description
00203001	Glyceryl Trinitrate tablet 0.5 mg	V	A	PHA	Tablet
00205801	Streptokinase for injection 1.5 MU vial	V	A	PHA	Vial
00404901	Disposable, IV giving sets	V	A	PHA	Set
00501502	Adrenaline/Epinephrin for injection 1 mg/1 ml ampoule	V	A	PHA	Ampoule
00602401	Anti Rabies Serum for injection 1,000 IU/5 ml ampoule	V	A	PHA	Vial
00401003	Sodium Chloride for IV Infusion 0.9%, 500 ml/bottle	V	A	PHA	Bottle
00401101	Dextrose injection 5%, 500 ml/bottle	V	A	PHA	Bottle
00701503	Hydrocortisone Sodi. succinate for injection, 100 mg vial	V	A	PHA	Vial
01500801	Atropine Sulphate for injection 600 mcg/1 ml ampoule	V	B	PHA	Ampoule
01501401	Suxamethonium Chloride for injection 100 mg/2 ml ampoule	V	B	PHA	Ampoule
01501901	Dantroline Sodium for injection 20 mg vial	V	B	PHA	Vial
00206901	Tenecteplase for injection 40 mg vial	V		PHA	Vial
00600204	Rabies Vaccine (Human use) 0.5 ml/1 ml -inactivated	V		PHA	Dose

IU = international unit; IV = intravenous; mg = milligram; ml = milliliter; MU = million units; PHA = pharmaceuticals; SRNO = serial number; VEN = Vital (V), Essential (E), Nonessential (N).

Notes:

1. The ABC analysis is one of the effective tools that applies drug consumption data over one year or a shorter period. It classifies pharmaceuticals into three categories: A, B, or C based on their total value (volume x unit price). Category A has the top 10%–20% of items that cover 70%–80% of cumulative value (cost). Category B covers 10%–20% of items with cumulative value of 15%–20%. Category C comprises 60%–80% of items with cumulative value of 5%–10%.
2. VEN analysis is a method that helps prioritize medicine purchase and stock keeping according to their health impact, whether vital, essential, or nonessential.

Source: Ministry of Health and the Asian Development Bank assessment team.

Top Most Required 25 Pharmaceuticals Based on Annual Monthly Forecast

SRNO	Item Description	VEN	ABC	Item Class	Unit Description
00700401	Metformin tablet 500 mg	E	A	PHA	Tablet
00206501	Atorvastatin tablet 10 mg	E	A	PHA	Tablet
00202901	Losartan Potassium tablet 50 mg	E	A	PHA	Tablet
00303301	Paracetamol tablet 500 mg	E	A	PHA	Tablet
00700301	Gliclazide tablet 40 mg	E	A	PHA	Tablet
00800802	Omeprazole capsule or tablet 20 mg	E	A	PHA	Capsule
00205404	Aspirin Enteric-coated tablet 75 mg	E	A	PHA	Tablet
00403401	Folic Acid tablet 1 mg	E	A	PHA	Tablet
00202301	Prazosin tablet 1 mg	E	A	PHA	Tablet
00501301	Chlorphenamine tablet 4 mg (Chlorpheniramine)	E	B	PHA	Tablet
00202601	Enalapril tablet 5 mg	E	A	PHA	Tablet
00205501	Clopidogrel tablet 75 mg	E	A	PHA	Tablet
00800401	Domperidone tablet 10 mg	E	A	PHA	Tablet
00200201	Hydrochlorothiazide tablet 25 mg	E	A	PHA	Tablet
00200301	Furosemide (Frusemide) tablet 40 mg	E	A	PHA	Tablet
00203301	Amlodipine Besylate tablet 5 mg	E	B	PHA	Tablet
01400302	Diclofenac Sodium tablet 50 mg	E	A	PHA	Tablet
00701701	Prednisolone tablet 5 mg	E	A	PHA	Tablet
00203501	Nifedipine ER tablet 20 mg	N	A	PHA	Tablet
00100101	Amoxicillin capsule 250 mg	E	A	PHA	Capsule
00501101	Cetirizine tablet 10 mg	E	B	PHA	Tablet
00500703	Beclomethasone DP capsule 400 mcg	E	A	PHA	Capsule
00304002	Sodium Valproate tablet 200 mg	E	A	PHA	Tablet
00500101	Salbutamol tablet 2 mg	E	A	PHA	Tablet
00701101	Thyroxine tablet 50 mcg	E	A	PHA	Tablet

mcg = microgram, mg = milligram.
Source: Ministry of Health and the Asian Development Bank assessment team.

Appendix 2: Good Storage Practices of Pharmaceutical Stores Assessed

The following are results gathered from the assessment of 82 stores.

	Practice Area	Fully Practiced	Partially Practiced	Not Practiced	Not Applicable
1	The facility has designated areas for reception zone, inspection zone, packing and delivery preparation zone, storage area, delivery zone, and office area.	4 5%	3 4%	75 91%	0
2	Storage area is secured with a lock and key, and is accessible during normal working hours with access limited to authorized personnel.	76 93%	6 7%	0 0%	0
3	Store area has sufficient space for storing and organizing different products for easy access, inspection, and counting. The current space and organization are sufficient for existing products and reasonable expansion (i.e., receipt of expected product deliveries in the foreseeable future).	24 29%	36 44%	22 27%	0
4	The storeroom is maintained in good condition (clean, all trash removed, sturdy shelves, organized boxes). Storeroom is cleaned and disinfected regularly. Storage area is visually free from harmful insects and rodents (there are no traces of droppings of rodents or insects).	42 51%	33 40%	5 6%	0
5	Storeroom is secured from the risk of water penetration and high humidity at all times of the day and during all seasons.	61 74%	13 16%	8 10%	0
6	Smoke detector, fire alarm, and fire safety equipment are available and easily accessible in the storeroom and personnel are trained to use them.	1 1%	1 1%	80 98%	0
7	Products are stored on pallets or shelves in a dry, well-lit, well-ventilated condition out of direct sunlight.	19 23%	38 46%	25 30%	0
8	Cartons are stacked at least 10 centimeters (cm) (4 inches) off the floor, 30 cm (1 foot [ft]) away from the walls and other stacks, and not more than 2.5 meters (8 ft) high.	4 5%	48 59%	30 37%	0
9	The facility maintains cold storage for vaccines, drugs, and commodities that require it.	46 81%	7 12%	4 7%	25
10	The storeroom temperature is controlled and monitored regularly with sufficient air-conditioning, thermometers, and temperature chart.	21 26%	30 37%	31 38%	0
11	Medical supplies are stored away from insecticides, chemicals, old files, office supplies, and other materials.	52 64%	19 23%	10 12%	1
12	Condoms and other latex products are stored away from electric motors and fluorescent lights.	25 83%	2 7%	3 10%	52

continued on next page

Table *continued*

	Practice Area	Fully Practiced	Partially Practiced	Not Practiced	Not Applicable
13	The facility keeps narcotics and other controlled substances in a locked place.	36	2	0	44
		95%	5%	0%	
14	The facility stores flammable products separately from other products and takes appropriate safety precautions for them.	47	11	21	3
		59%	14%	27%	
15	The facility separates damaged and expired products from the regular stock and disposes them as per guidelines.	37	34	9	2
		46%	43%	11%	
16	The facility uses location codes and shelf labels for easy allocation and management of storage location for products.	15	29	38	0
		18%	35%	46%	
17	There are bin cards attached to the stack of products. Cartons are arranged so that arrows point up, and identification labels, expiry dates, and manufacturing dates are clearly visible.	2	5	75	0
		2%	6%	91%	
18	The facility rotates the supply, organizes stock, and dispenses products on a first expiry first out manner.	80	0	2	0
		98%	0%	2%	
19	The facility has a policy for minimum and maximum stock of a product to prevent stock out or overstock.	3	12	67	0
		4%	15%	82%	
20	The facility maintains stock cards; inventory movement records (for receipt, registration and storage, and dispatch of products); and produces periodic warehouse and inventory reports.	54	19	9	0
		66%	23%	11%	
21	The facility makes it a practice to conduct sample stock count, spot count, and full stock count on a periodic basis.	66	13	3	0
		80%	16%	4%	
22	The facility uses a warehouse management information system or logistics management information system.	48	7	27	0
		59%	9%	33%	
23	The facility minimizes the risk of loss of quality of products during transportation to other facilities or end users by ensuring that the products are transported under ideal temperature, free from direct sunlight and water.	65	4	4	9
		89%	5%	5%	
24	The facility conducts periodic stock analysis by using previous distribution data to calculate average monthly consumption and forecast current stock level.	50	10	22	0
		61%	12%	27%	
25	Staff in charge of the store have clearly assigned job description and are trained on storage, distribution, and inventory management.	40	11	31	0
		49%	13%	38%	

Source: Data collected through the store assessment visits.

SELECTED REFERENCES

P. Galappatthy et al. 2021. WHO/INRUD Core Drug Use Indicators and Commonly Prescribed Medicines: A National Survey from Sri Lanka. *BMC Pharmacol Toxicol*. 22 (67).

A. U. Gamage and C. Abeysena. 2020. Health Technology Assessment (HTA) and Health Policy Making: A Narrative Review. *Journal of the College of Community Physicians of Sri Lanka*. 26 (1).

Government of Sri Lanka. 2014. *National List of Essential Medicines, Sri Lanka, 2013–2014, Fifth Revision*. Ministry of Health.

Government of Sri Lanka. 2018. *National Health Performance Framework*. Ministry of Health.

A. L. Guyer. 2021. *Procurement of Medicines in Sri Lanka: A Case Study*. Harvard School of Public Health.

P. John and S. Khemani. 2023. Best Practices in Procurement and Supply Chain Management Systems for Medicines. *Working Paper*.

W. Prosser et al. 2021. Designing Supply Chains to Meet the Growing Need of Vaccines: Evidence from Four Countries. *Journal of Pharmaceutical Policy and Practice*. 14 (80).

G. S. P. Ranasinghe, P. W. C. Panapitiya, and S. M. Samarage. 2021. Strengthening the Drug Supply Chain Management in a Tertiary Care Hospital in Sri Lanka. *International Journal of Scientific and Research Publications*. 11 (6, June). pp. 22–35.

P. Ranasinghe et al. 2022. National Survey on World Health Organization/International Network of Rational Use of Drugs Core Drug Use Indicators in the Outpatient Setting and Availability of Medicines in a Developing South Asian Country. *Journal of Pharmaceutical Health Services Research*. 3 (2, June). pp. 158–65.

D. Rathish et al. 2017. Availability of Essential Medicines in Selected Public, Primary and Secondary Health Care Institutions of a Rural Sri Lankan District: A Spot Survey. *BMC Health Services Research*. 17 (11).

Save The Children. 2014. *Pharmaceutical Supply Chain*.

E. Settanni et al. 2017. Pharmaceutical Supply Chain Models: A Synthesis from a Systems View of Operations Research. *Operations Research Perspectives*. 4. pp. 74–95.

O. Smith. 2018. Sri Lanka: Achieving Pro-Poor Universal Health Coverage Without Health Financing Reforms. *Universal Health Coverage Study Series*. No. 38. World Bank Group.

J. Snow, Inc./DELIVER. 2005. Logistics Indicators Assessment Tool (LIAT). John Snow, Inc./ DELIVER for the United States Agency for International Development.

Sri Lanka Association of Clinical Pharmacology and Therapeutics. Evidence Synthesis on Essential Medicines Policy Reform Options for Sri Lanka. World Health Organization (Project No. 2022/1279296-0).

B. B. Tefera and G. T. Anbessa. 2022. Pharmaceutical Supply Chain Practices and Its Associated Factors in Public Health Facilities, West Gojjam Zone, Ethiopia: Cross-Sectional Study. *Hosp Pharm*. 57 (5, Oct). pp. 622–632.

The National List of Essential Medicines, Sri Lanka. 4th revision.

P. Thekkur et al. 2022. Primary Health Care System Strengthening Project in Sri Lanka: Status and Challenges with Human Resources, Information Systems, Drugs and Laboratory Services. *Healthcare*. 10 (2251).

United Nations Children's Fund. 2019. Technical Review of Public Health Supply Chain Assessment Tools: An Analysis of Major Tools and Approaches.

United States Agency for International Development. 2009. Logistics System Assessment Tool (LSAT). USAID Deliver Project, Task Order 1.

J. Wijayasiriwardhana. 2020. Study on Issues of Drug Availability and Recommendations of Improving the Availability in Health Care Institutions of Sri Lanka. *World Journal of Pharmaceutical Research*. 9 (15). pp. 127–138.

J. L. H. R. Wijegunasekara. 2021. Drug Supply Management in Health Care Institutions in Sri Lanka: A Case Study. *Journal of Drug Delivery and Therapeutics*. 11 (1). pp. 3–7.

World Bank Group. *Universal Health Coverage Study Series (UNICO)*. No. 38.

World Health Organization (WHO). 2007. Everybody's Business—Strengthening Health Systems to Improve Health Outcomes: WHO's Framework for Action.

———. 2018. *System Design Approach to Improve the Immunization Supply Chain.*

P. Yadav. 2017. *25 Years of Health Product Supply Chain Reform: Market Forms of Organization Versus Public Ownership.* William Davidson Institute, University of Michigan.

www.ingramcontent.com/pod-product-compliance
Lightning Source LLC
Chambersburg PA
CBHW041756220926
51847CB00014B/224
9789292772338